JOHN SINGER SARGENT

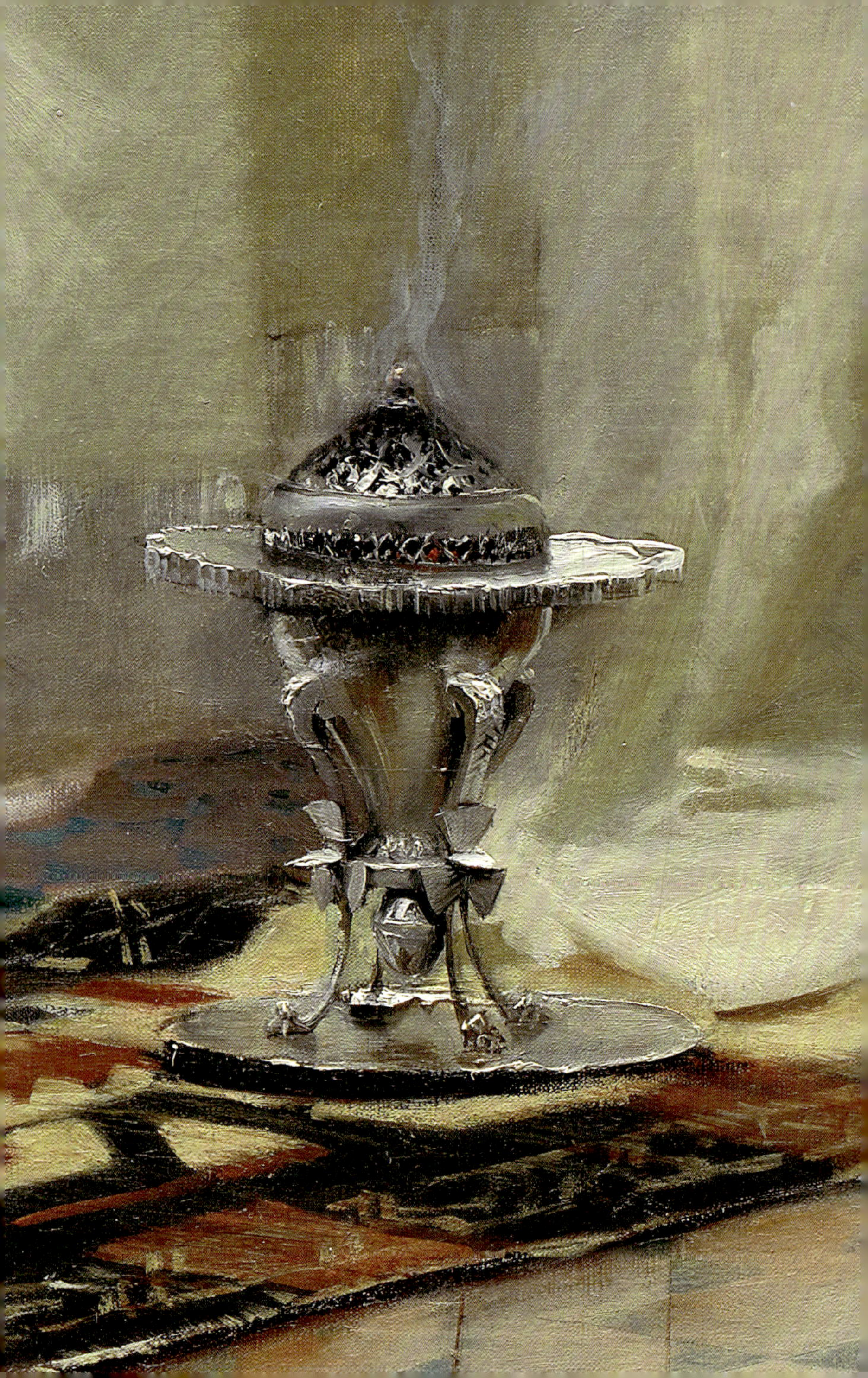

JOHN SINGER SARGENT

ELIZABETH PRETTEJOHN

TATE

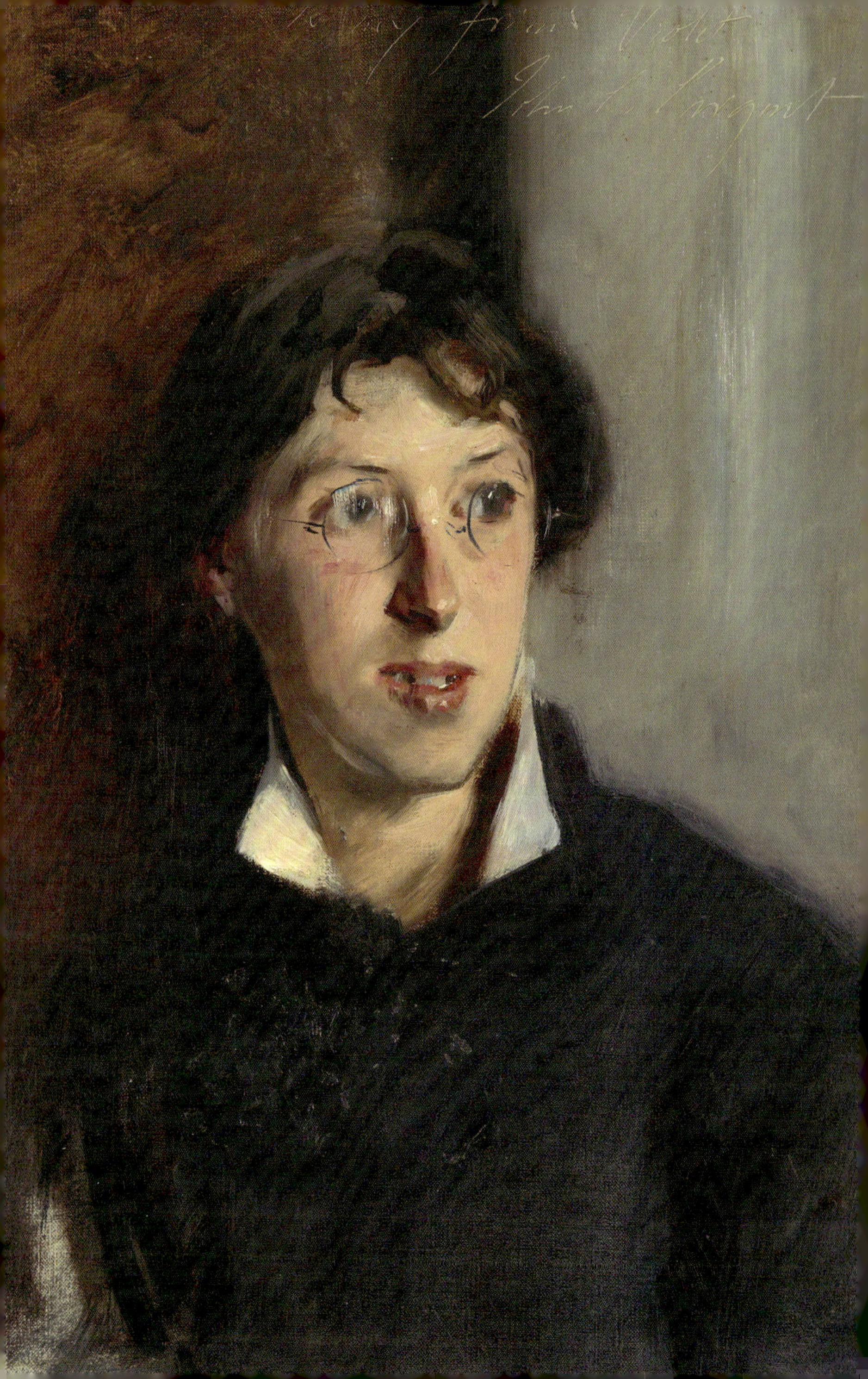

On 23 June 1881, when Sargent painted his childhood friend Violet Paget, she was about to publish her second book on Italian art and aesthetics, under the gender-neutral pseudonym by which she is still best known, Vernon Lee. Although Sargent's portrait is a rapid sketch, made in a single sitting, it adroitly captures the personality of the sitter, brimming with intellectual energy (opposite). As Lee put it herself, in a letter to her mother: 'It is of course mere dabs & blurs & considerably caricatured, but certainly more like me than I expected anything could [be] – rather fierce and cantankerous.'[1] Viewing the portrait, we feel we are encountering the writer in vivid actuality, glasses glinting, mouth slightly open as if about to speak. Her hairstyle and attire – black silk with a crisp white collar – match her pseudonym in refusing to conform to either a masculine or a feminine stereotype. Perhaps Sargent was alluding to his friend's sexual preference for women.[2] Certainly he was acknowledging her intelligence and the seriousness of her commitment to her career as a writer.

All this is evoked with supreme economy, in broad strokes that seem to conjure the living head out of a mere blur of neutral colours. The portrait sketch therefore makes a fitting introduction to Sargent's work, not only for its compelling characterisation of the sitter, but also for the pictorial means by which he achieves this result. There was no time, on that day in 1881, for the kind of finish that would be expected of a commissioned portrait. Yet the head is fully modelled as a three-dimensional volume in a strong light from the right, which modulates into deep shadow on the other side of the face without losing relief against the barely sketched background. The solid structure of the head is so confidently established that it takes nothing more than a flick of the brush to delineate an eyebrow, a pink dab to form a lower lip. The viewer's suspension of disbelief does the rest of the work needed to make the complete set of facial features materialise in all immediacy. A photograph of the sitter might provide much more accurate detail, but it could never persuade us, as the sketch does, that we are in the living presence of Vernon Lee herself.

ernon Lee 1881
il paint on canvas
3.7 × 43.2

A COSMOPOLITAN CHILDHOOD

Vernon Lee and John Singer Sargent were exact contemporaries, born in 1856 to cosmopolitan families. They met as children in the 1860s when both families were living in Nice, and were later reunited in Rome. Sargent's doctor father was from Gloucester, Massachusetts and his artistic mother, an amateur watercolourist, from Philadelphia, but in 1854, after the death in early childhood of their first daughter, the Sargents moved to Europe. Of their five children born in subsequent years only three lived to maturity: John, born in Florence, Emily (born in Rome in 1857) and Violet (born in Florence in 1870). Amidst these vicissitudes of births and deaths, the Sargents were constantly on the move. Winters were usually spent in Rome, Florence or Nice, and summers in cities, resorts and spas in Switzerland, Germany, France or Italy. The family were intrepid as well as inveterate travellers; in 1868, for example, they made an extended trip to Spain, still considered a difficult and dangerous destination

Sargent was proud to be American, but he did not even visit his native land until he was twenty years old, and never lived there. In his childhood he had no permanent home at all. After his father relinquished his medical career, the family lived on a moderate independent income, and the need for economy was one reason for their restlessness. Yet their temporary lodgings offered abundant opportunities for novel experiences and delights. Vernon Lee later recalled dinner parties in the Sargents' rented apartment above the Spanish Steps in Rome, with its views of St Peter's Basilica and its strange medley of furnishings, including marble busts of George Washington and the Egyptian goddess Isis.[3] Sargent's painting of his sister Violet as a teenager shows the breakfast table of lodgings in Nice, adorned with shining silver and glassware, roses and fresh white linen; a fashionable Japanese print hangs on the wall behind the figure (opposite). His youthful letters show him already a seasoned, as well as avid, gallery-goer in his teens, and one who knew his art history. At age thirteen he is in raptures over ancient statues in the Glyptothek, Munich; before he reaches twenty he is recounting his recent passion for Tintoretto.[4]

This strange, peripatetic childhood can scarcely have been good for the young Sargent's general education, and for the rest of his life he was apt to display gaps in his basic knowledge. It was, however, a life of constant and endlessly

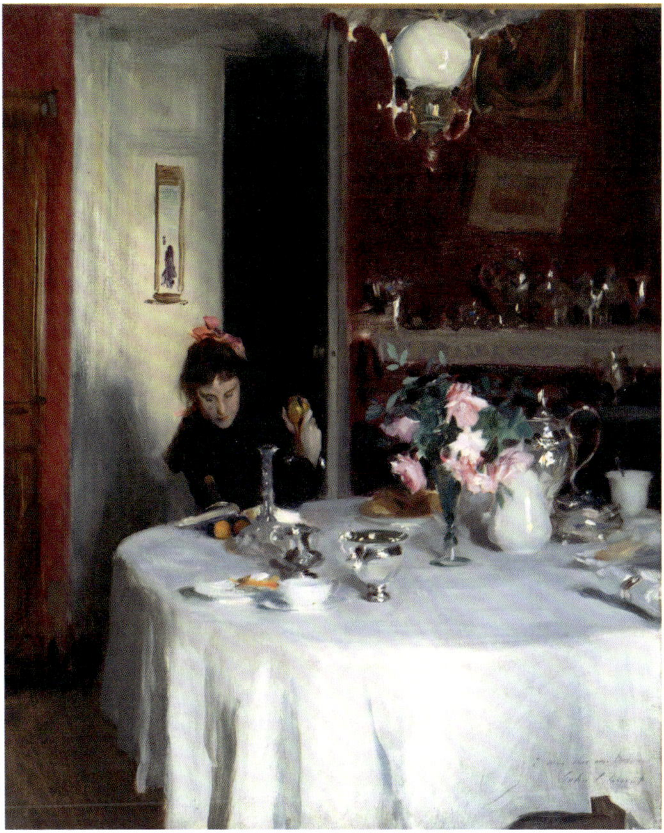

iolet Sargent or
he Breakfast Table c.1883
il paint on canvas
5.2 × 46.3

varied visual stimulation. His own letters, and others' accounts of him, show that the boy Sargent was constantly drawing everything he saw around him – scenery, artworks, animals, and people of all kinds. Perhaps the frequent changes in his environment can be seen as formative for his later artistic practice, his flair for capturing a distinctive moment in all its vivid immediacy.

Sargent's parents came from solidly respectable American middle-class backgrounds and would have had little experience of art as a profession. His father was a Puritan and a patriot, and seems to have hoped, for a time, that his son would be attracted to a career in the US navy, much in the news in the aftermath of the American Civil War of 1861–5. But the Sargents were also art-lovers, and remarkably open-minded. As it became increasingly clear that their son was at his

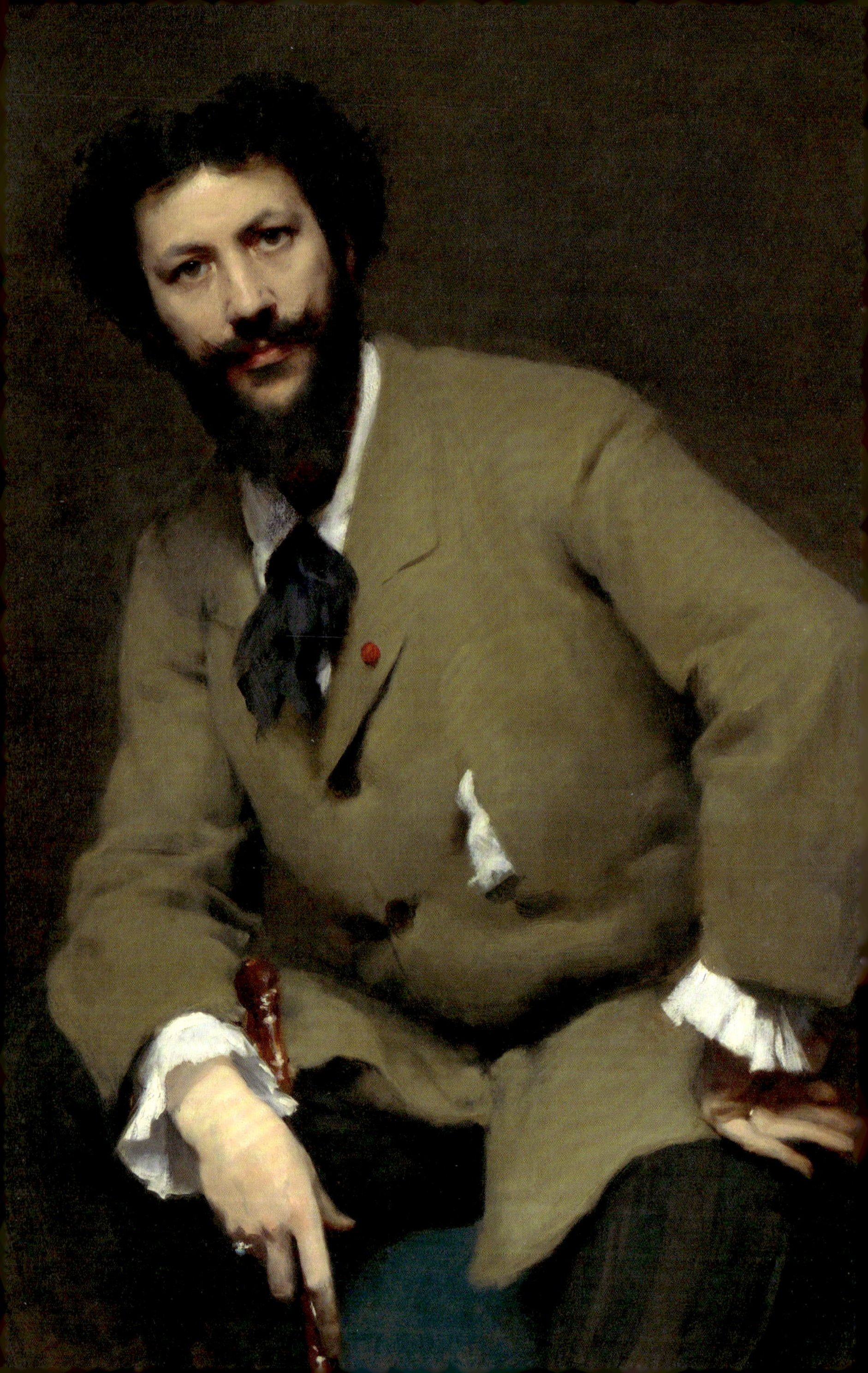

happiest, and most industrious, when drawing, they reorganised their travels to make opportunities for his artistic education. After a brief stint at the Accademia delle Belle Arti in Florence, the eighteen-year-old Sargent arrived with his family in the foremost centre for artistic training in the world: Paris.

AROLUS-DURAN THE ART WORLD PARIS

The Sargents arrived in Paris on 16 May 1874 – intriguingly, the day after the end of the first group exhibition of the artists whom critics were beginning to call 'impressionists'. Sargent would later explore the novel styles of these artists and form a close friendship with the leading impressionist, Claude Monet (p.44). For the moment, however, his sights were set on a more basic training, which he pursued with exceptional rigour. He enrolled in the private teaching studio of Carolus-Duran (the professional name of Charles-Émile-Auguste Durand), a recently fashionable studio particularly popular with American students. Sargent also passed the difficult entrance examinations for the state-funded École des Beaux-Arts, where he quickly gained a reputation for skill and flair in drawing. In 1877, his third set of exams for the École, he won second place, a record both for an American and for a student of Carolus-Duran. That year he also made his debut at the Salon, the principal, state-sponsored annual exhibition in Paris.[5] In the remarkably short space of three years, Sargent had made the shift from promising art student to fully fledged professional. Two years later he consolidated his success with a portrait of his teacher, Carolus-Duran, which won an Honourable Mention at the Salon of 1879 (opposite).

These early achievements (and indeed the choice of Carolus-Duran, himself a highly successful portraitist, both as teacher and as sitter for this key work) suggest that Sargent already had in mind a career in portraiture, a sensible choice for a young American whose family were still nervous about his chances of earning a living. By agreeing to sit for his talented pupil – a time-consuming task, and one bound to attract critical attention – Carolus-Duran was effectively ratifying the plan. Even at this early date, however, there are signs that Sargent was less interested in career advantage than in the creative potential of portrait-painting, and his sitter seems to have been prepared to collaborate. The portrait abandons the upright pose and staid demeanour normally expected

ırolus-Duran 1879
il paint on canvas
6.8 × 95.9

in portrayals of prominent men. Instead, the figure swerves to the side, so that his head appears dramatically left of centre The rest of the body is arrayed on dynamic diagonals, one elbow akimbo, the other hand elegantly extended to grasp a slender cane, also at an angle. Already Sargent is alert to how dress can contribute to the design and characterisation of a portrait. The unstructured coat, its texture miraculously conveyed by the brushwork, establishes the volume of the bod and its positioning within the picture space. Ruffled cuffs, the edge of a handkerchief and a loose tie give just a hint of artistic dandyism, with which the bright red note of the buttonhole – in fact a status symbol, the ribbon of the Légion d'Honneur – seems surprisingly to concur. The carefully groomed mustachios and neatly parted hair follow suit. And yet the first, and lasting, impact of this portrait is in the powerful stare with which the sitter rivets our attention. Carolus-Duran, as painted by Sargent, refuses to recede into a respectable distance, as in so many traditional male portraits. He seems to require us to return his gaze.

In the next few Salon exhibitions, Sargent followed this success with further experiments in portraits of increasing scale and ambition, as though he were testing the modern potential of each of the traditional portrait types – from the full-length figure in the out-of-doors (p.32) to groups of children (pp.39, 41). He was not, however, prepared to be typecast as a portraitist, and he simultaneously showed pictures of the people and places he encountered on the travels that, in Sargent family fashion, he continued to pursue – to the coast of Brittany (pp.26, 28–9), Capri and the Bay of Naples (pp.30, 31), Spain (pp.36–7), and Morocco (p.35). Each painting, whether it is a portrait or a subject picture, is a fresh experiment in artmaking. Now in his later twenties, the American artist was still finding his style, even as he was building up an impressive record of Salon successes, and burgeoning critical acclaim.

PORTRAIT DE MME***

The culmination of this carefully orchestrated rise to fame was a major statement: a full-length formal portrait in the grand manner tradition, like the portraits of royalty and aristocracy familiar since the Renaissance (opposite). But the portrait was not a commission, and the sitter was no aristocrat Like Sargent himself, she was an American making her way

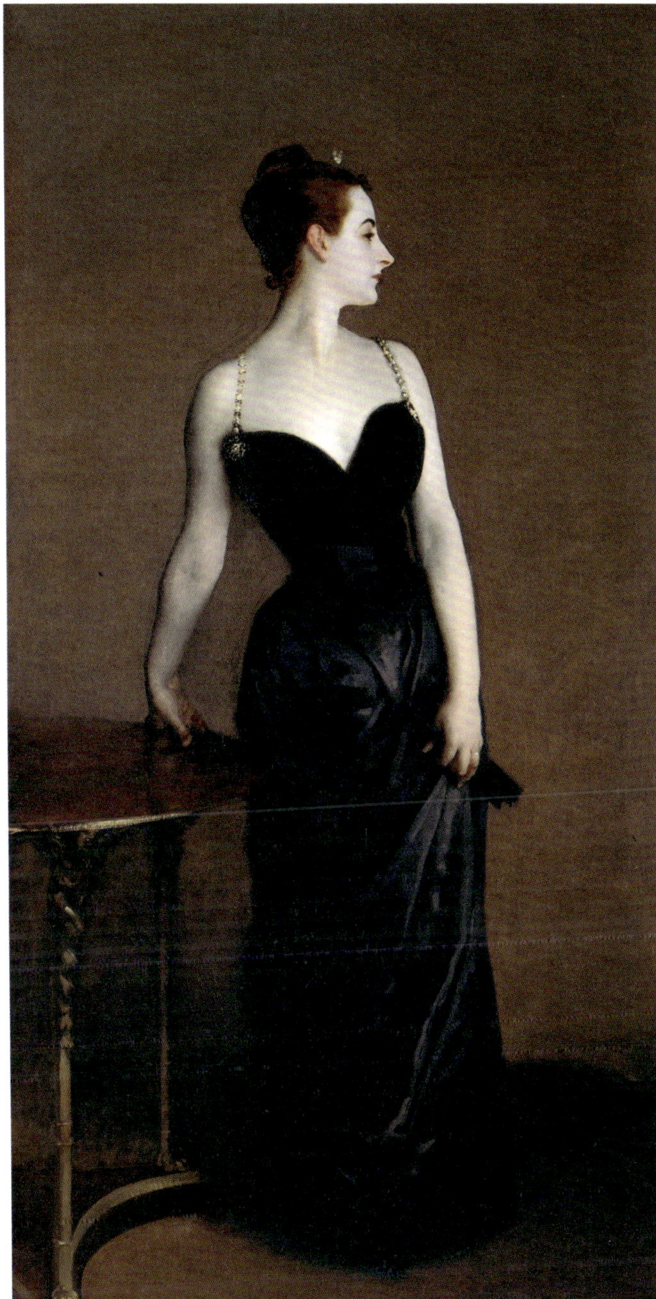

adame X or Madame
autreau 1883–4
il paint on canvas
08.6 × 109.9

into the European elite: born Virginie Avegno in Louisiana, she became Madame Pierre Gautreau on her marriage to a Parisian banker. Sargent was fascinated by her 'beautiful lines' and the artificial colour of her made-up skin, which he described as 'uniform lavender or blotting paper colour all over'.[6] Although the portrait appeared at the Salon exhibition in 1884 with the anonymous title, *Portrait de Mme ****, critics readily identified the figure as a 'professional beauty' – a recognisable social type, brought to perfection in Sargent's supremely elegant presentation.

Recent technical examination has shown how carefully Sargent developed the lines of this composition, making numerous changes to the positioning of the head and arms.[7] Miraculously, the final result appears clean and perfect – the head in pure profile, the arms starkly outlined against the dark dress and background.[8] When the portrait appeared at the Salon, the reaction from public and critics was immediate and intense. The critic for the redoubtable art journal, the *Gazette des Beaux-Arts*, reported on the crowds that gathered before the painting, and their outraged exclamations 'Détestable! Ennuyeux! Curieux! Monstrueux!'[9]

This was a classic *succès de scandale* – in one sense, an endorsement of the still young American painter's rise to preeminence at the world's leading exhibition venue. But if it was a triumph, it was an uncomfortable one. Sargent had taken a risk, but there was risk for Virginie Gautreau too, something of which he was acutely aware. As his friend Ralph Curtis reported, '[Madame] Gautreau and [her mother] came to [Sargent's] studio "bathed in tears." I stayed them off but the mother returned and ... made a fearful scene saying "Ma fille est perdue – tout Paris se moque d'elle..."' ('My daughter is lost – all Paris is mocking her'). Sargent stood his ground, insisting that 'nothing could be said of the canvas worse than had been said in print of her appearance'.[10]

Sargent may have been taken aback by the public and critical response to the painting, but he knew that he had created a significant work, and after the Salon exhibition was over he displayed it conspicuously in his Paris studio. However, he was always a considerate and tender-hearted man, as countless anecdotes demonstrate. He refrained from selling the painting until after Virginie Gautreau's death, and even then tactfully requested that her identity should not be revealed to the press – hence the title under which the painting is now famous: *Portrait of Madame X*. But Sargent remained confident about the painting's quality, and the purchaser was the foremost art institution in the home country of both sitter and artist, the Metropolitan Museum of Art in New York. As he told the Director: 'I suppose it is the best thing I have done.'[11]

NGLAND AMERICA

Sargent's biographers have sometimes claimed that the scandal over the portrait of Virginie Gautreau caused him to flee to London, and there may be a kernel of truth in this. However, he was already widening his artistic horizons beyond Paris. Indeed, he was a leader in the rapid internationalisation of the art world that was so conspicuous in the later nineteenth century, stimulated by the great international exhibitions from London's Crystal Palace exhibition of 1851 onwards. This development gathered pace in the 1880s, with added impetus from a flourishing American art market, and Sargent, along with his fellow American James Abbott McNeill Whistler, was at the forefront.

In 1882, Sargent had made his debut at the Royal Academy exhibition, London's counterpart to the Paris Salon, with a striking full-length portrait of the French surgeon and gynaecologist Dr Samuel Jean Pozzi, resplendent in a brilliant red dressing gown (p.40). Within the next few years he also began to show work at new exhibiting venues in London: the Grosvenor Gallery, stronghold of the aesthetic movement, and (from its inception in 1886) the New English Art Club, an association of younger artists with leanings towards France. Meanwhile, Sargent was also a leader in the rapidly developing US art world: he participated in the new Society of American Artists in New York from its first exhibition in 1878. And he never lost his connection with Paris, even after moving away; he continued to show work not only at the Salon but also at newer exhibitions such as those of the Société internationale des peintres et sculpteurs, a notably international grouping of artists, held at the Galerie Georges Petit. In the later 1880s, he made his most searching explorations of impressionism, inspired by his friendships with French artists (pp.44–6, 51). Sargent's career connects all these art world centres, traditional and new.

Despite all his travels, Sargent had never lived in an

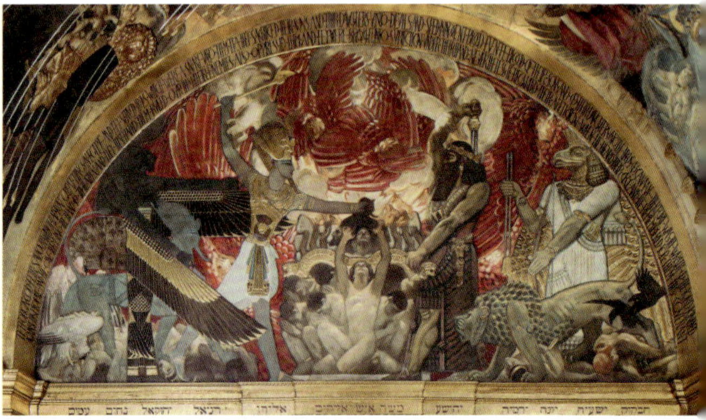

The Children of Israel Beneath the Yoke of their Oppressors, installed 1895
Oil paint on canvas with relief elements of gilded papier-mâché and plaster
336.6 × 674.4

English-speaking country, and it was only after his thirtieth birthday that he struck roots in both England and America. The great American novelist Henry James (p.88) played an important role in both developments: he encouraged Sargent to move to England, where he had himself been resident since 1876. In 1887, he also published a reflective article on Sargent's work in the widely read New York monthly *Harper's Magazine*, effectively introducing the artist to the American public just before the first of his working journeys to the United States.

In 1886 Sargent moved to a studio in Tite Street, formerly occupied by his compatriot Whistler and in the heart of artistic Chelsea, in southwest London. Sargent finally had a home, for the first time in his life. From 1891 his mother and sister maintained a flat in one of the newly fashionable blocks nearby, Carlyle Mansions. In 1900 Sargent leased the adjoining house in Tite Street, which more than doubled his living and studio space – by Sargent family standards, this was permanence. Yet he never gave up the habit of travel, which remained a source of creative refreshment throughout his life. As he put it: 'The only pleasure of coming back to one's own house is the pleasure of unpacking the *bibelots* one has got elsewhere.'[12]

Meanwhile he also established himself in his native country – never as a resident, but on extended journeys in 1887–8 and again in 1889–90. One purpose of these trips was to fulfil the portrait commissions that quickly began to proliferate. In 1890, however, Sargent also received the commission to execute mural paintings for an important public building, the new Boston Public Library designed by the leading architectural firm McKim, Mead & White. After some deliberation he settled on an ambitious theme, 'The Triumph of Religion', elaborated on the walls and ceilings of a large barrel-vaulted hall, with impressive groups of paintings at either end representing Jewish (opposite) and Christian religious history.[13] This project, together with further mural commissions for the Boston Museum of Fine Arts and Harvard University's Widener Library, occupied much of Sargent's time and energy for the remaining thirty-five years of his life. Although they have never been as well known as his portraits and subject paintings, the murals deserve attention as important expressions of a new American confidence in monumental artmaking, designed to rival the great public art projects of the European tradition since the Renaissance.

The establishment of Sargent's London studio and his US journeys initiated his heyday as a painter of commissioned portraits, which lasted until 1907, when he finally succeeded in enforcing his determination to scale back his portrait practice. 'No more paughtraits', he wrote to his friend Ralph Curtis, the jokey spelling perhaps parodying an upper class accent; 'I abhor and abjure them and hope never to do another especially of the Upper Classes.'[14] To satisfy his importunate clients, he turned to making rapid charcoal head studies, which eventually numbered over seven hundred (p.78). His creative urge, along with his compulsion to travel, remained undiminished, and resulted in hundreds of watercolours of varied places and people in his later years (pp.71, 81, 86, 87, 89).

Although Sargent is often classified as a 'society painter' (and sometimes with condescension), that is far too simple a description. At the time he was painting, the 'upper classes' were in a state of significant flux, and Sargent's sitters came from a dizzying variety of backgrounds – imperial administrators (p.74) and industrialists (or their families, pp.42–3), doctors and social activists (pp.40, 64), celebrity actors (p.49), writers and musicians (p.52), as well as titled or high society figures (pp.56, 61, 62, 65, 92), and Americans, whose social mobility could seem unnerving, from old Bostonians (p.73) and heiresses (pp.48, 53) to artists' families (p.54) and presidents (p.72).[15]

For a time it might have seemed that Sargent's modern style appealed principally to the nouveaux riches or the artistically adventurous. Soon enough, though, the traditional ruling classes joined the queue of those eager to be painted by him. An intriguing example is *The Marlborough Family* of 1904–5 (p.75) – the portrait of a hereditary aristocrat, the Ninth Duke of Marlborough, with his wife and children (and their dogs), designed to hang opposite the magnificent grand-manner portrait of a previous Marlborough family, painted by Sir Joshua Reynolds in the late 1770s, at Blenheim Palace, the family seat in Oxfordshire. But the Duke's wife was Consuelo Vanderbilt, heiress to a new American fortune. Sargent was documenting the changing kaleidoscope of the international elite. More than that: he was creating their visual image. *Lord Ribblesdale* of 1902 seems to represent the quintessential British aristocrat (p.70) – but, at the time of painting, this was a class that was widely seen to be in decline, and perhaps that idea is just perceptible in the figure's excessive, though elegant, leanness.

SARGENT'S JEWISH SITTERS

A significant subset of Sargent's sitters were of Jewish heritage. Sargent had a special affinity for Jewish sitters, perhaps because he identified with their position apart from mainstream society; many Jewish families shared the Sargents' rootlessness, although for different reasons.

His portraits capture a distinctive moment in their social history, after Jewish people had won civil and political rights throughout much of Europe, but before the significant backlash of the twentieth century. That backlash, most notorious in Nazi Germany, is also evident in the critical fortunes of Sargent's portraits. Beginning in 1898, the London art dealer Asher Wertheimer commissioned twelve portraits of himself and his family – the largest group of portraits Sargent ever painted (pp.57, 68, 69, 79). For a decade, as he joked to Lady Lewis, another Jewish friend, he was in a state of 'chronic Wertheimerism'.[16] When nine of the portraits were bequeathed to the national art collection of Britain, some critics hailed them as the artist's greatest achievement. However, there were also accusations that the Wertheimers were attempting to insinuate themselves into excessive prominence in the national collection – a classic antisemitic slur.[17] Sargent shows the Wertheimers, who became close friends, at the height of their success and prosperity, but his own reputation may have been tarnished in the increasingly

Mrs Carl Meyer and her Children 1896
Oil paint on canvas
209.9 × 135.9

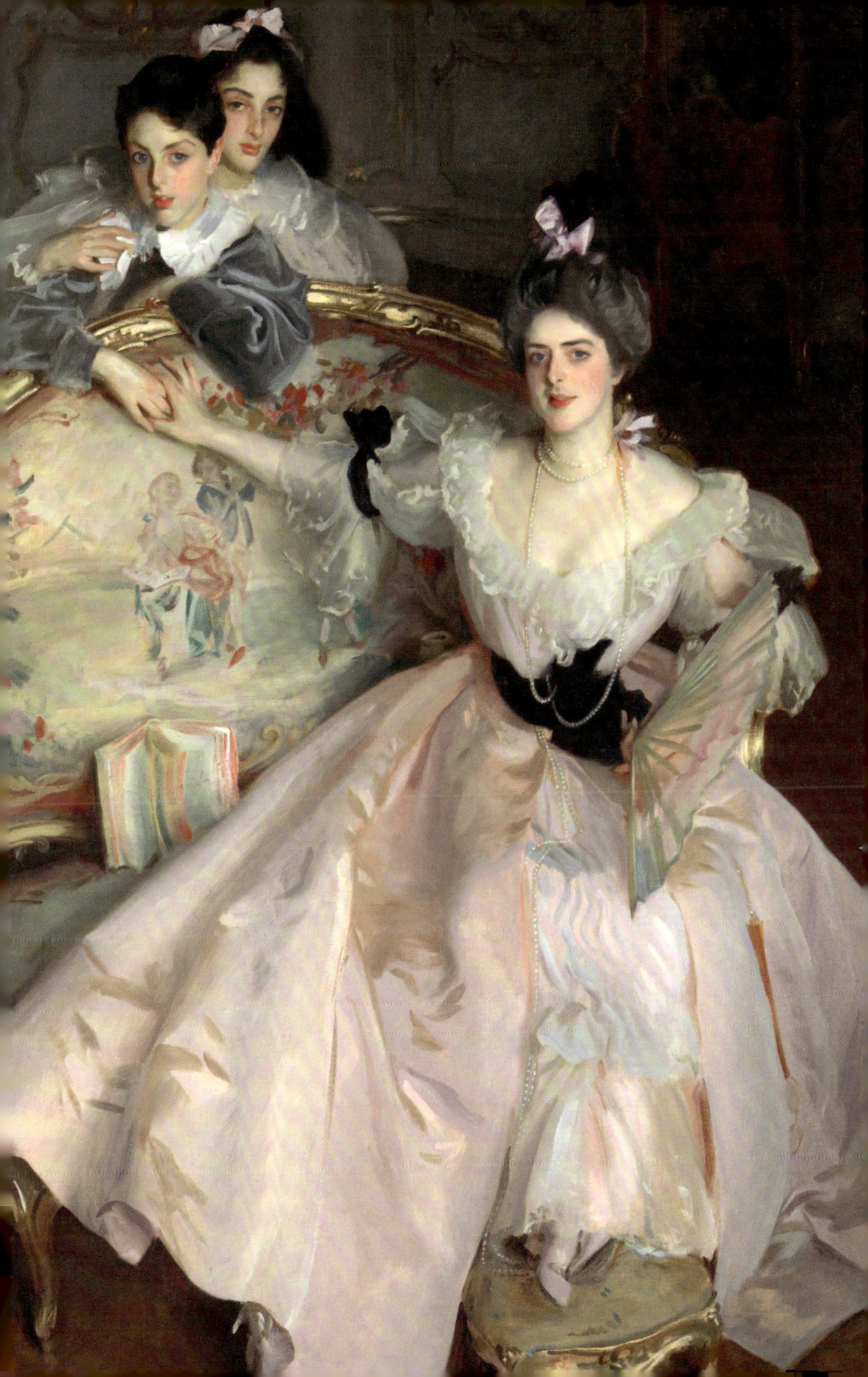

xenophobic climate of the early twentieth century. The full set of Wertheimer portraits was discreetly removed from display, and it was only in 2022 that they reappeared on the walls of Tate Britain as a complete group.

Sargent's rapport with his Jewish sitters resulted in some of his most adventurous paintings, such as *Mrs Carl Meyer and her Children*, exhibited at the Royal Academy in 1897 (the year before the first Wertheimer commission) (p.17). Adèle Meyer, a generous patron of the arts and advocate of women's suffrage, was prepared to allow Sargent to represent her with a flamboyance that seems almost to verge on satire. Her pose and billowing costume recall the portraits of Madame de Pompadour, also a distinguished patron of the arts, by the eighteenth-century painter François Boucher, and she is surrounded by French Rococo accoutrements: gilded panelling in the style of Louis XV, a sofa and footstool adorned with Beauvais tapestry. These antiques were so sought-after in the later nineteenth century that only someone of immense wealth, such as Mrs Meyer, could afford them. Extravagant ropes of pearls loop twice around her neck, drop to her bodice and down her peach-pink skirt, finally to fall next to her tiny pink slipper, perched as if weightless on the gilded stool at her feet. The two children, like Mrs Meyer herself, were immediately legible to art critics as Jewish, and some of the reviews of 1897 seem tinged with antisemitism, whether deliberate or inadvertent. Yet the critical responses, even when hostile, acknowledge something important about Sargent's painting: what Henry James called the 'knock-down insolence' with which he gave his sitters glamour and verve without disguising their Jewish identities.[18]

FRIENDSHIP

Portrait painting is an intensely sociable activity, and Sargent was no loner. On his multifarious travels later in life he was accompanied by an entourage of friends, relations and fellow artists – not to mention the elaborate paraphernalia of his painting practice, including billows of textiles and other props (even, on one occasion, a stuffed gazelle). Sargent's friendships are intertwined in complex ways with his portrait practice. Some sitters for commissioned portraits – such as the Wertheimers – became close friends. Other friends became subjects for portraits.[19] The quality of aliveness that critics from Sargent's day to now have found in his best

elf-Portrait 1906
)il paint on canvas
0 × 53

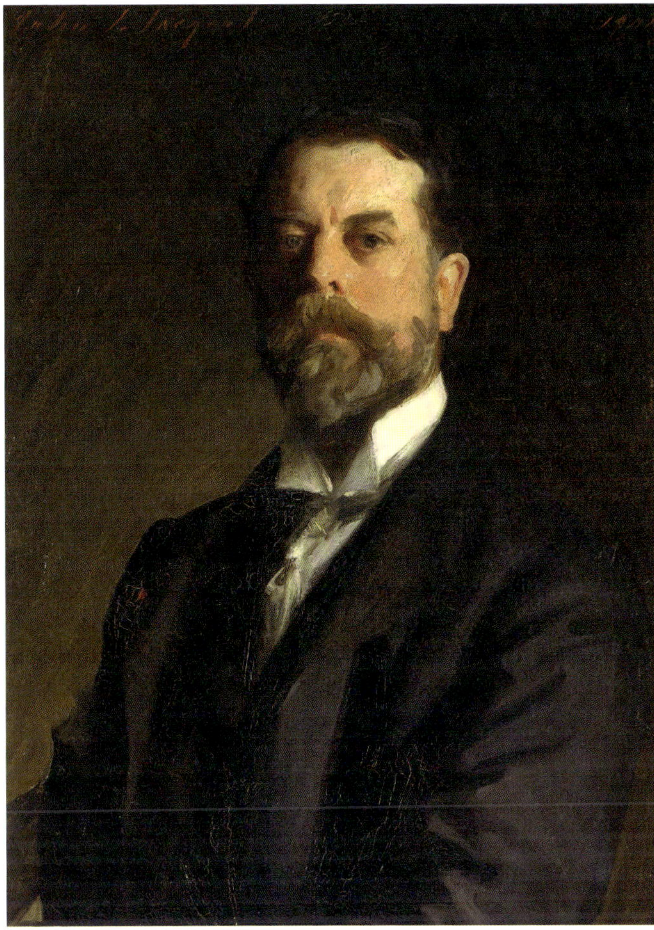

portraits can be attributed, at least in part, to the engagement Sargent felt with the people represented. It mattered less whether or not they were paying for the portrait than whether the spark of friendship emerged between sitter and painter. When it did, the result could be electrifying. Sargent's self-portraits – not energised by friendship with another person – tend to be among his least adventurous images (above).

When Sargent visited the novelist Robert Louis Stevenson (author of *Treasure Island* and *The Strange Case of Dr Jekyll and Mr Hyde*) and his American wife, born Fanny Osbourne, at their house in Bournemouth, he was inspired to make what might be called a friendship portrait of both of them (p.20). 'Anybody

Robert Louis Stevenson and his Wife 1885
Oil paint on canvas
52.1 × 62.2

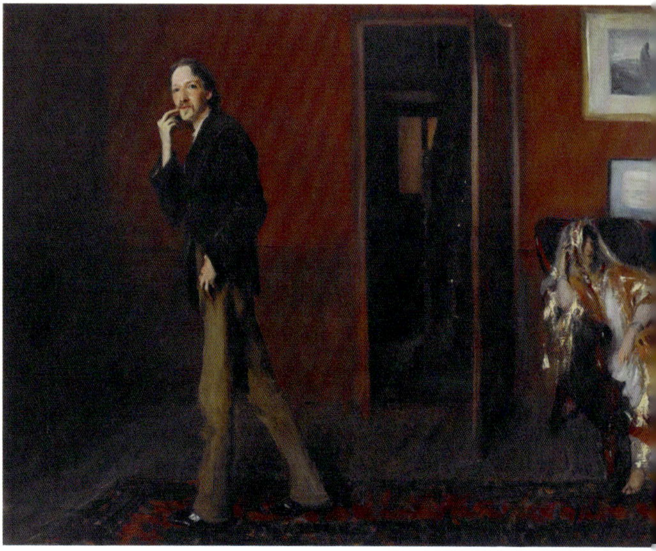

may have a "portrait of a gentleman"', as Fanny wrote, 'but nobody ever had one like this. It is like an open box of jewels.' Sargent was inspired to include Fanny by her dress: 'the robes (veritable) of an Indian princess, one blaze of gold and colour and white lace'. The portrait was the subject of affectionate banter between artist and writer. Sargent referred to it as 'the picture of the caged animal lecturing about the foreign specimen in the corner' and loaned it to another friend, the art critic and curator Sidney Colvin, who wrote to yet another writer friend, W.E. Henley: 'Have you seen Sargent's picture? It's him to the life in gesture and expression – living life, with a touch of charge'.[20] By 'him', Colvin means Stevenson, the sitter, but the phrase could equally apply to the artist: the double portrait, made quickly on inspiration, epitomises Sargent's way of painting, 'to the life'.

Sargent was a skilful pianist and music-lover, and many of his closest friendships were with musicians, among whom a particular favourite was the French composer Gabriel Fauré (p.52). As the Australian-born composer Percy Grainger noted: 'Two things stand out in my memory of [Sargent] – his unfailing benevolence where the welfare of art was concerned, and his inscrutability in all that touched his purely personal life.'[21] Nothing is known of Sargent's romantic or sexual life, such a closely guarded secret that we can

ude Study of Thomas
. McKeller c.1917–20
il paint on canvas
25.7 × 84.5

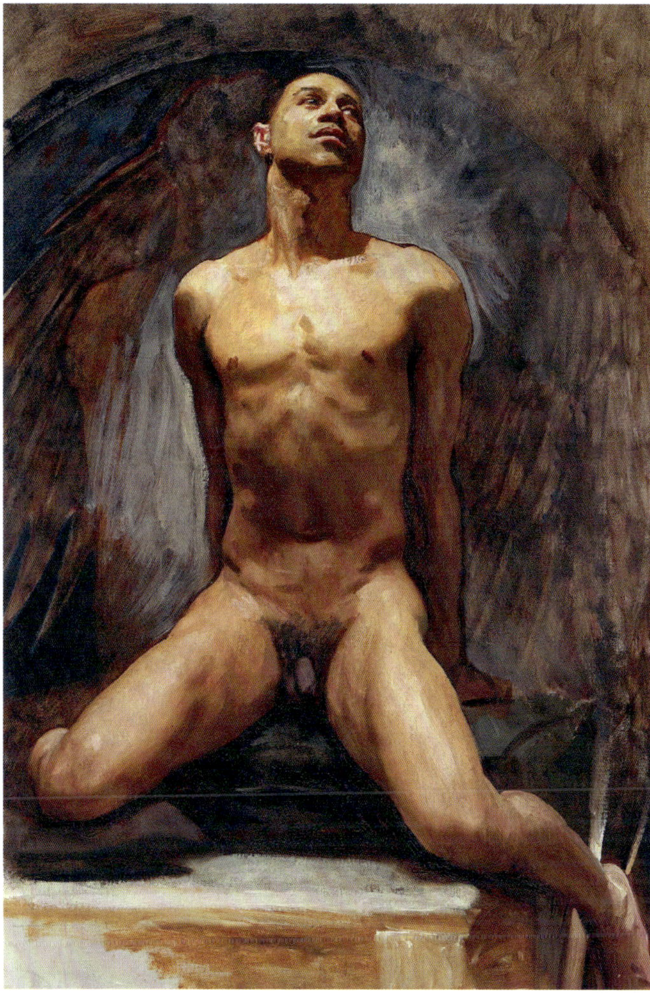

be certain that he did not wish it to be a topic of discussion. As demonstrated in important recent research by the art historian Trevor Fairbrother, however, Sargent's paintings and drawings reveal a keen sensual engagement with certain male figures and more generally with the male body.[22] This is seen most compellingly in his oil study of an African-American model, Thomas E. McKeller (above).

Sargent's sensual, or even erotic, engagement with the people he was painting – women as well as men – was closely related to the sensuousness of his handling of painting materials, and to his love of beautiful things. Above all, he took delight, both tactile and visual, in all aspects of fashion, textiles and fabrics: as well as Fanny Stevenson's Indian robes, the jewels and iridescent beetle wing cases sewn into Ellen Terry's costume as Lady Macbeth (p.49),[23] the cashmere shawls he took on alpine painting expeditions (p.80) and every variety of silk, satin, velvet, chiffon, tulle and lace.[24]

STUDIO PRACTICE & TECHNIQUE

Not only was Sargent's clientele much more varied than the designation 'society painter' might suggest; portraiture, for him, was never a mere matter of pleasing the client and collecting his fee, but always an adventure in artmaking. Henry James put this succinctly in his seminal article on the artist: for Sargent, the work was 'not only a portrait, but a picture'. James described the visible effect of Sargent's working procedure in non-technical terms: 'The process by which the object seen resolves itself into the object pictured is extraordinarily immediate. It is as if painting were pure tact of vision, a simple manner of feeling.'[25]

Sargent was taught in Carolus-Duran's studio to paint with decisiveness, to model the entire form directly on the canvas, with attention above all to the values of light and dark. In his workaholic early years, he developed the technical facility that enabled him, later, to sustain a prodigious output. He was an avid student of the art of the past, and learned most from the old masters who painted rapidly – from Tintoretto, Hals and Velázquez (particularly recommended by Carolus-Duran; see p.34 for a spirited copy after Velázquez) to Gainsborough and Lawrence.[26] These direct and rapid methods must partly have been temperamental, but they were also expedient. It was no longer acceptable to have a team of assistants to paint the costumes and accessories, as the eighteenth-century portraitists routinely had. Nor was it possible to obtain dozens of sittings from busy celebrities, grandees or plutocrats. Sargent needed to paint fast, and the lessons of the old masters were crucial in forming his style.[27] This could enable feats of virtuosity which seemed like magic to those who observed them in the studio; one sitter recalled 'seeing Mr. Sargent paint my scarf with one sweep of his brush'.[28]

When asked to describe his technique by the artist John Collier, who named Sargent 'by far the most commanding

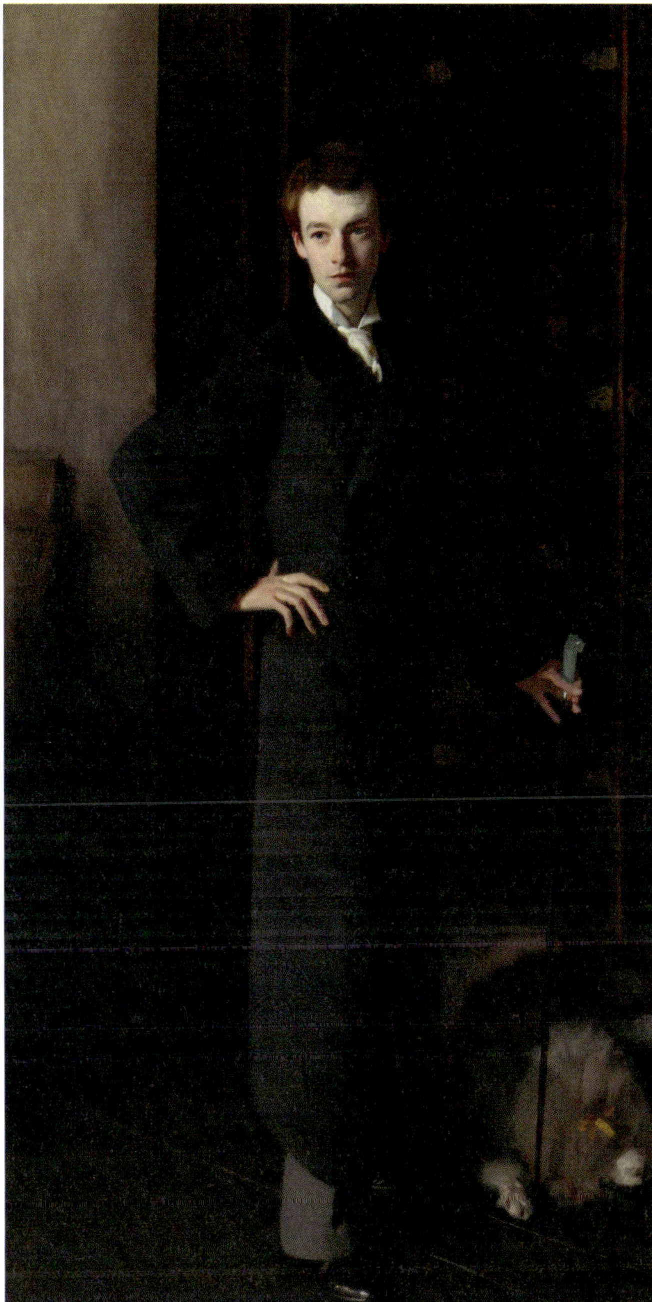

Graham Robertson 1894
l paint on canvas
0.5 × 118.7

figure in modern portraiture' in his book *The Art of Portrait Painting* (1910), Sargent confessed himself unable to put it into words.[29] Fortunately, some of his students provided accounts of what he taught them, principally by demonstration. 'You want plenty of paint to paint with', he told a young American student, Julie H. Heyneman. But the well-loaded brush should be used with confidence and verve: 'the fewest strokes possible to express a fact'.[30] It was essential to establish the entire structure of the head before painting in the facial features. Sargent was notorious for darting backwards and forwards as he worked, to gauge the effect of the image from a distance. 'Stand back – get well away – ... keep the thing as a whole in your mind', he told the students in the Royal Academy Schools.[31]

The painter and writer Walford Graham Robertson has left an engaging account of sitting for his portrait by Sargent (p.23). 'In 1894 I blossomed into a Notable Personage myself: it was a second-hand notability, a reflected aureole but distinctly noticeable... I became the subject of one of John Sargent's most famous pictures.' This is the Englishman's self-deprecation, and yet it also hints at why the portrait is more than just a likeness, more also than the coalescence of the social type of the artist as dandy. A few pages later Robertson makes hilarious play of his travails with his overcoat in a hot summer: '"But the coat is the picture", said Sargent. "You must wear it."'[32] Self-deprecating again – it is the coat, and not the man, who makes the portrait – but it also makes sense in relation to the painting: the portrait might itself be called self-deprecating. The vulnerability of the youthful figure, bathed in such a cold light, and so thin that the lines of his coat fall straight as a die, gives a compelling sense that we are seeing a human being.

THE FIRST WORLD WAR & SARGENT'S FINAL YEARS

August, 1914: inevitably, Sargent was on a painting expedition with friends in the Austrian Tyrol, when war was declared. At first, he seems to have regarded the war with some irritation as an interruption to his ability to travel freely, although nothing could stop him finding new scenes to paint. In the summer of 1916, while visiting the US to complete the installation of his Boston Public Library murals, he took his painting holiday in Glacier Park, Montana, and the Canadian Rocky Mountains (p.89). When the tragic consequences of

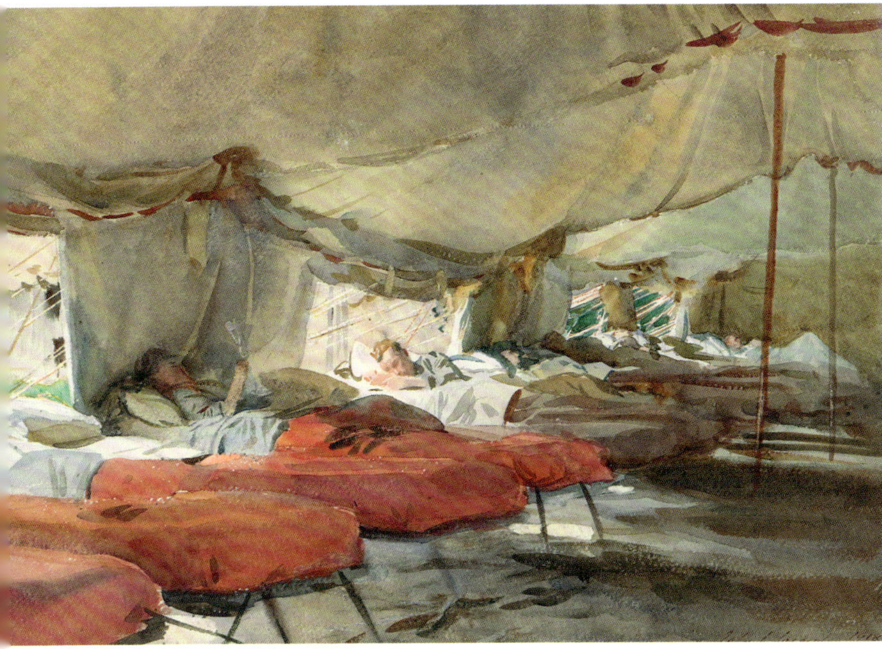

the war became apparent, he negotiated a commission as official war artist and travelled to the front in France. The principal result was *Gassed* (pp.90–1), a grand and moving portrayal of soldiers blinded by a mustard gas attack, based on a scene Sargent witnessed in August 1918. His experiences at the front were also captured in numerous sketches and watercolours such as *The Interior of a Hospital Tent* (above), a surprisingly beautiful evocation of the treatment of wounded soldiers in a makeshift tent illuminated by radiant sunlight. His irrepressible need to draw or paint, evident since childhood, remained with him throughout the war and to the end of his life.

On the evening of 14 April 1925, he served as host for a dinner at his sister Emily's flat in Carlyle Mansions. The next day he was due to depart for Boston to install the last of his Museum murals. But when the servant came to wake him for the journey, he was found to have died in his sleep. Sargent died as he had lived: in the middle of a painting project, and about to embark on a new journey. In the words of his friend Vernon Lee: 'The summing up of a would-be biographer must, I think, be: *he painted*.'[33]

he Interior of a Hospital
ent 1918
/atercolour on paper
9.3 × 52.8

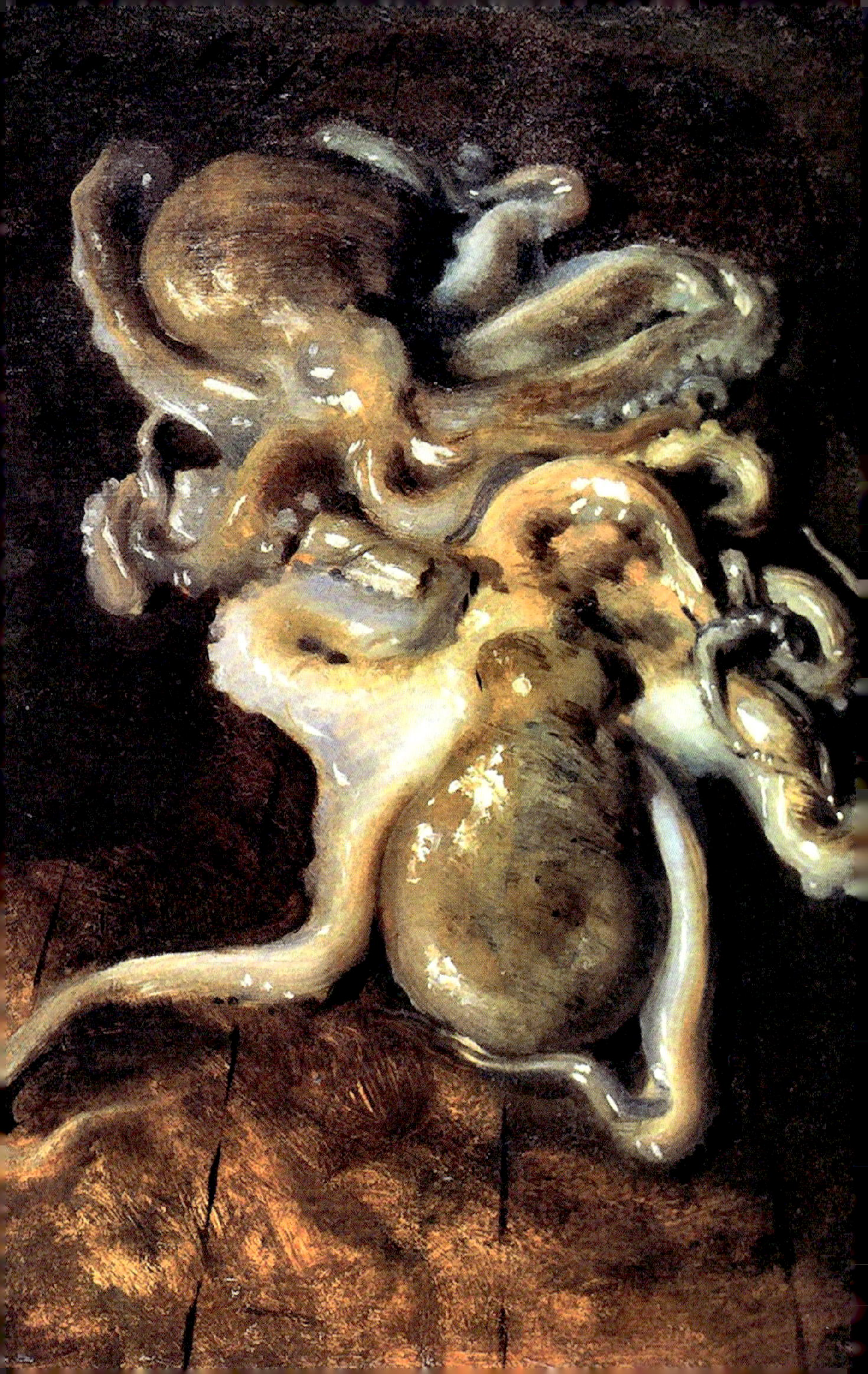

vo Octopi c.1875
il paint on canvas
).6 × 32.1

VERLEAF
yster Gatherers of Cancale
377–8
il paint on canvas
) × 123.2

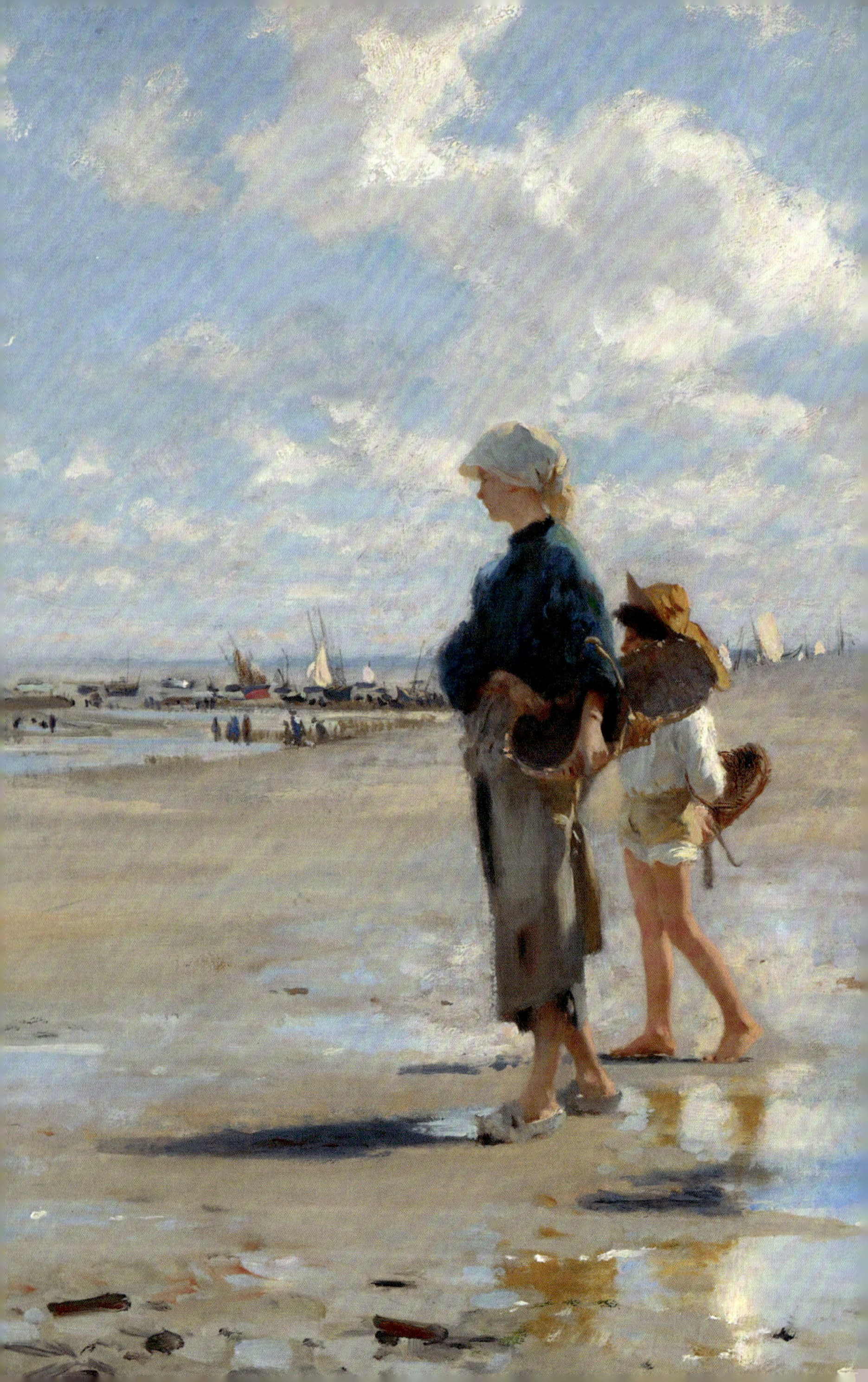

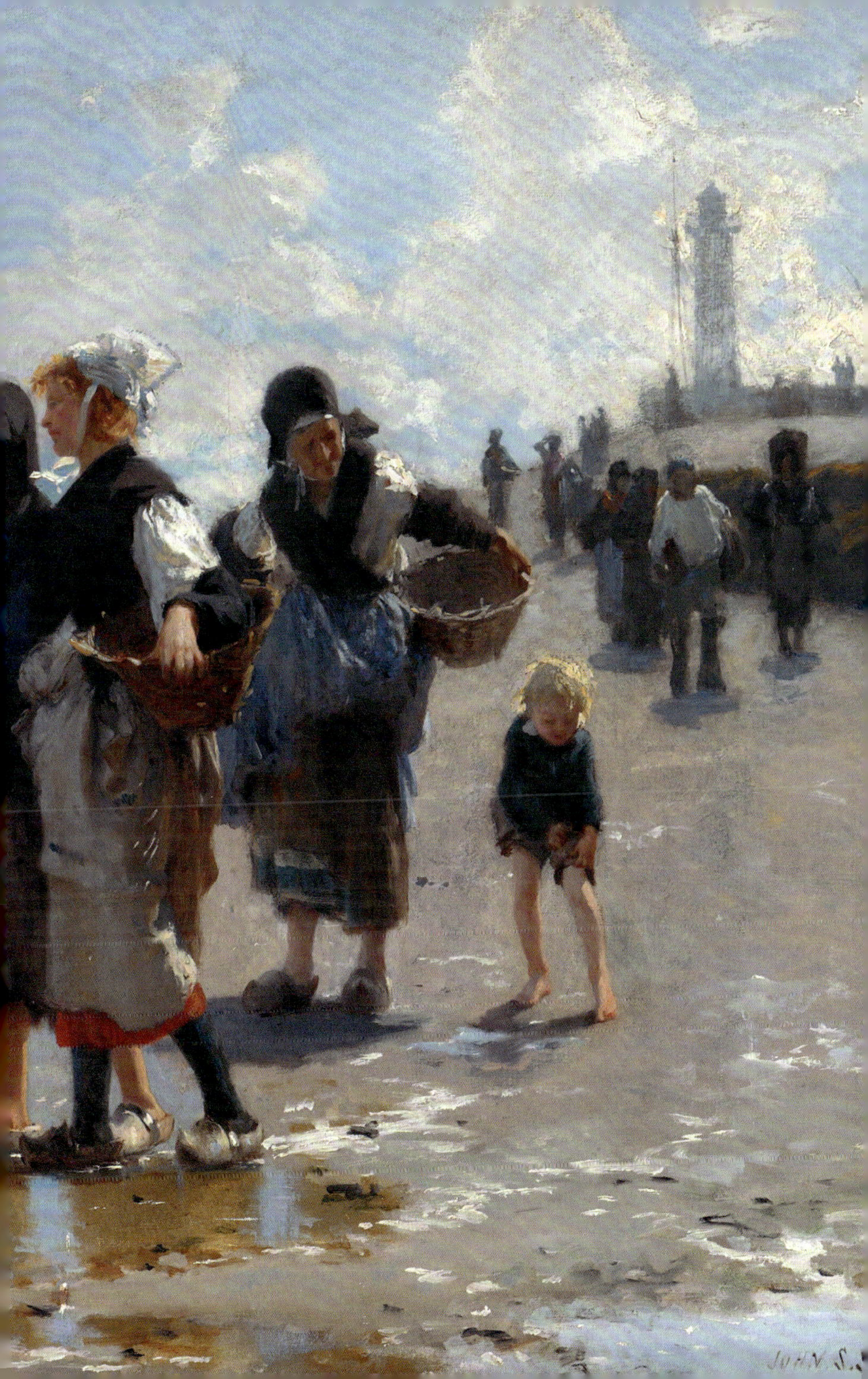

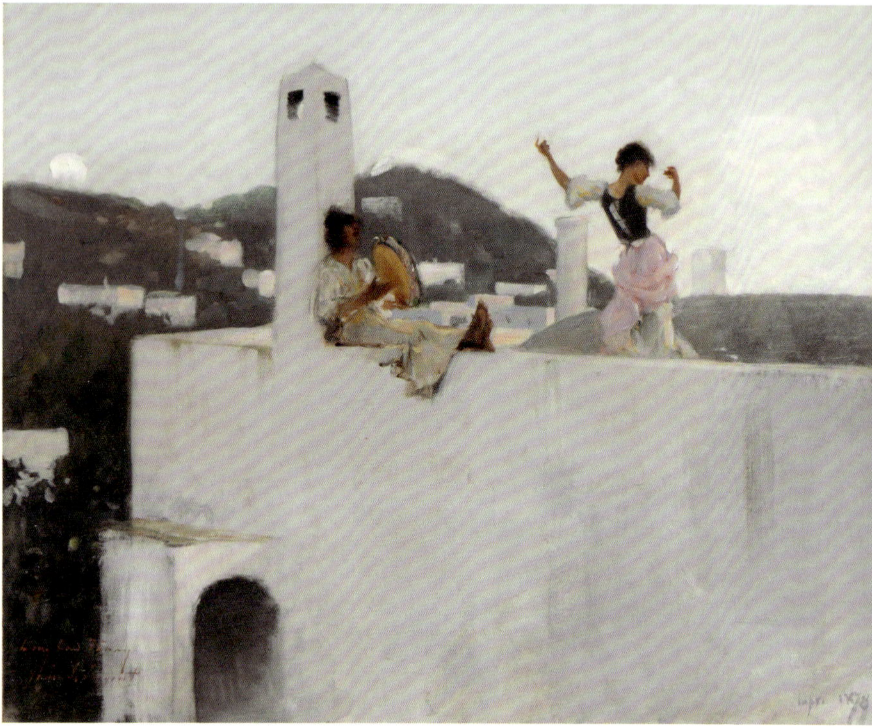

Capri Girl on a Rooftop 1878
Oil paint on canvas
50.8 × 63.5

Neapolitan Children Bathing
1878–9
Oil paint on canvas
26.8 × 41.1

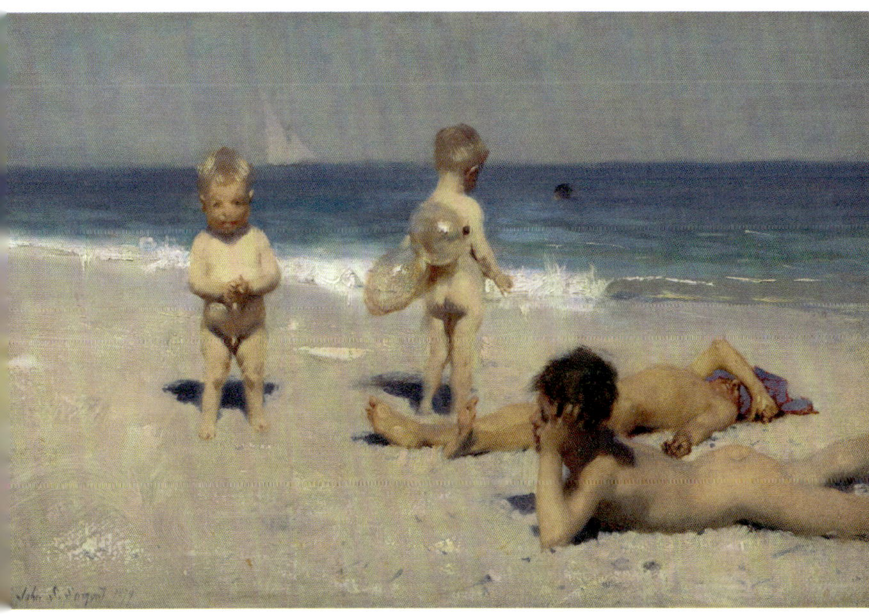

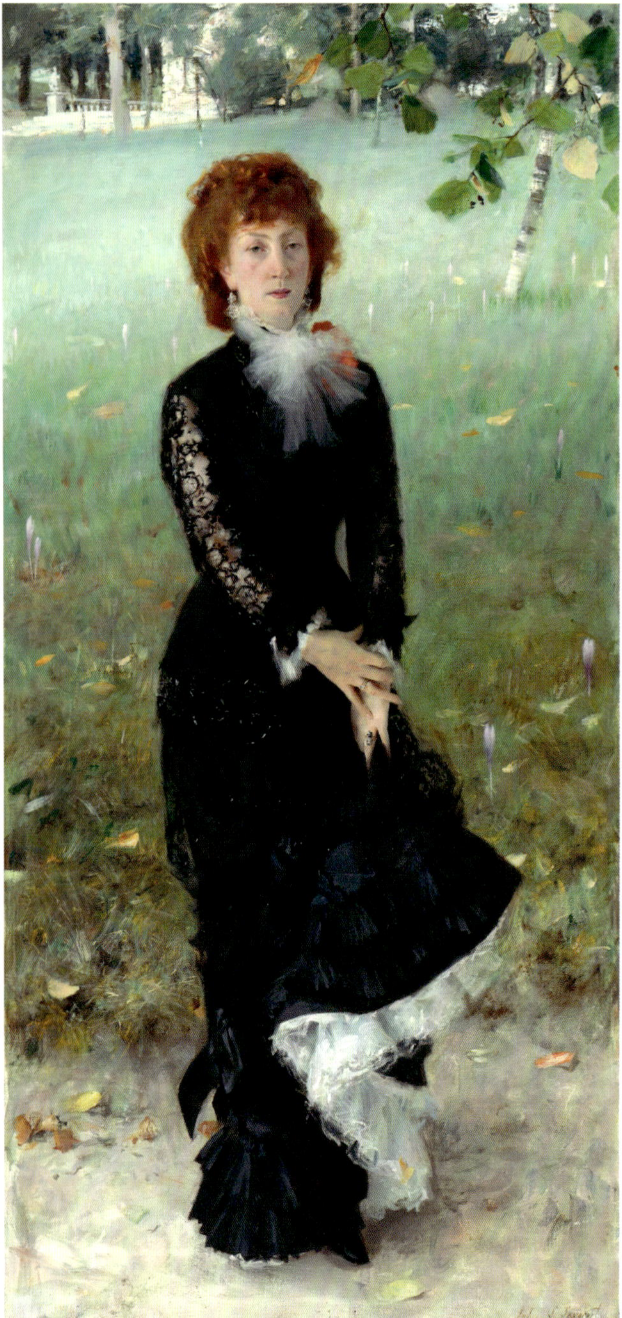

Madame Édouard Pailleron
1879
Oil paint on canvas
208.3 × 100.3

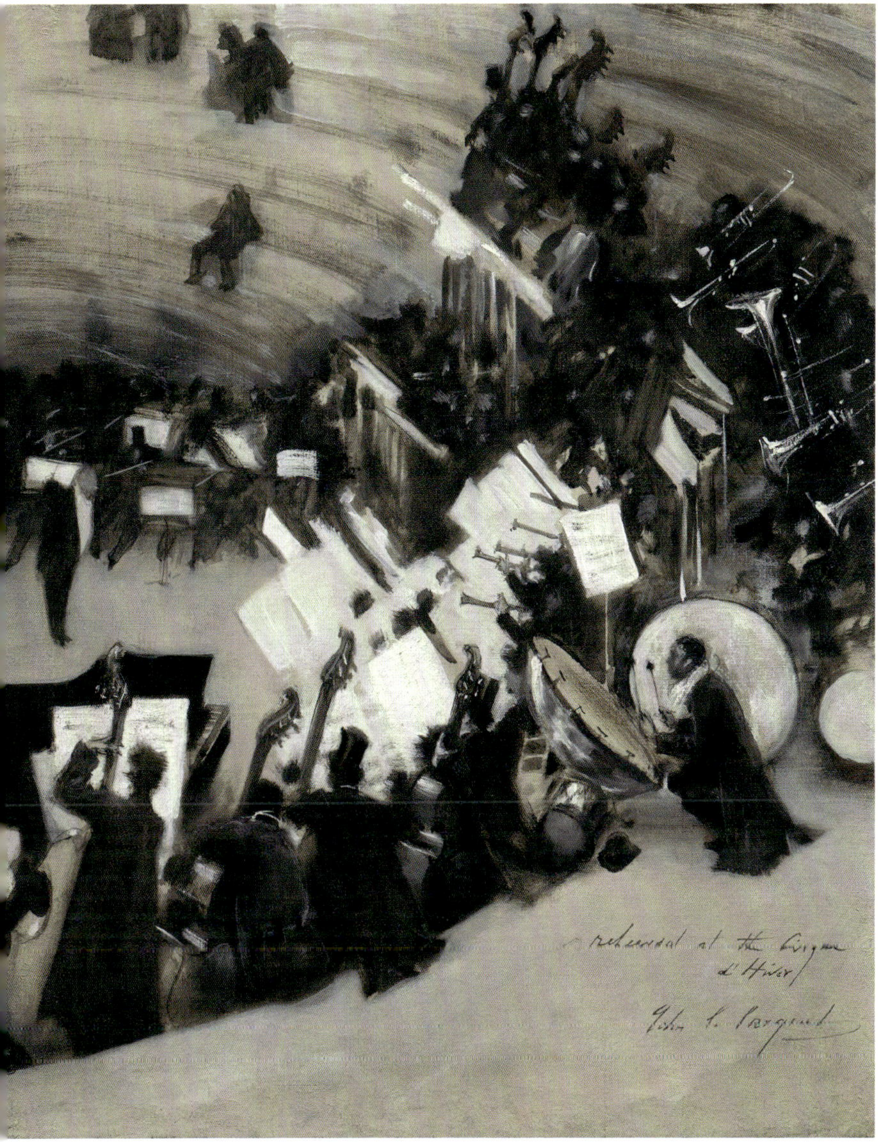

earsal of the Pasdeloup
hestra at the Cirque d'Hiver
879
paint on canvas
2 × 46

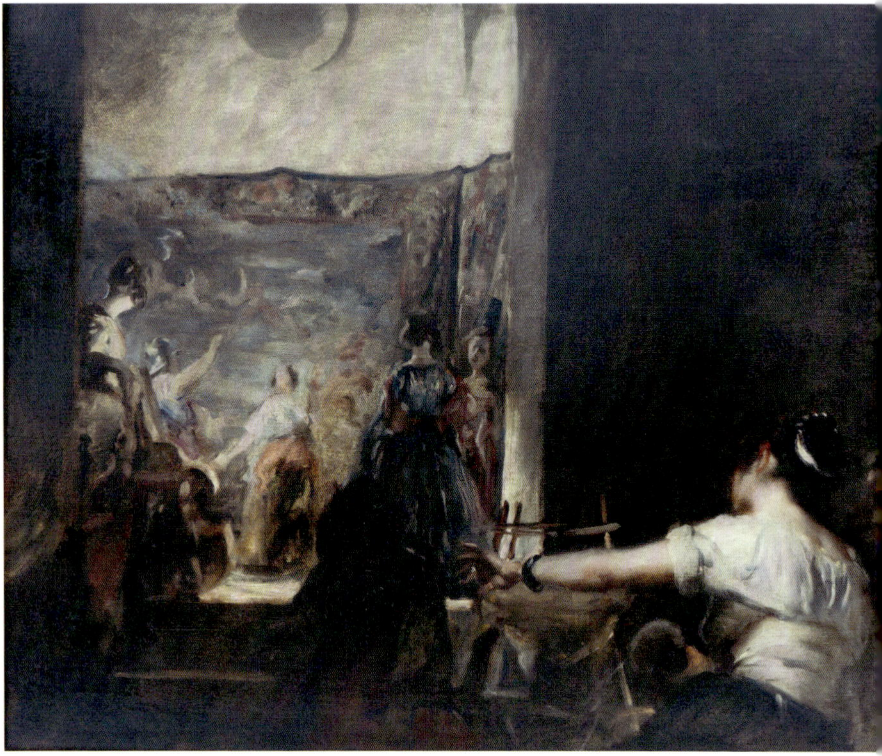

Las Hilanderas, after Velázquez
1879
Oil paint on canvas
58.4 × 71.1

OPPOSITE
Fumée d'ambre gris 1880
Oil paint on canvas
139.1 × 90.6

OVERLEAF
El Jaleo c.1880–2
Oil paint on canvas
237 × 352

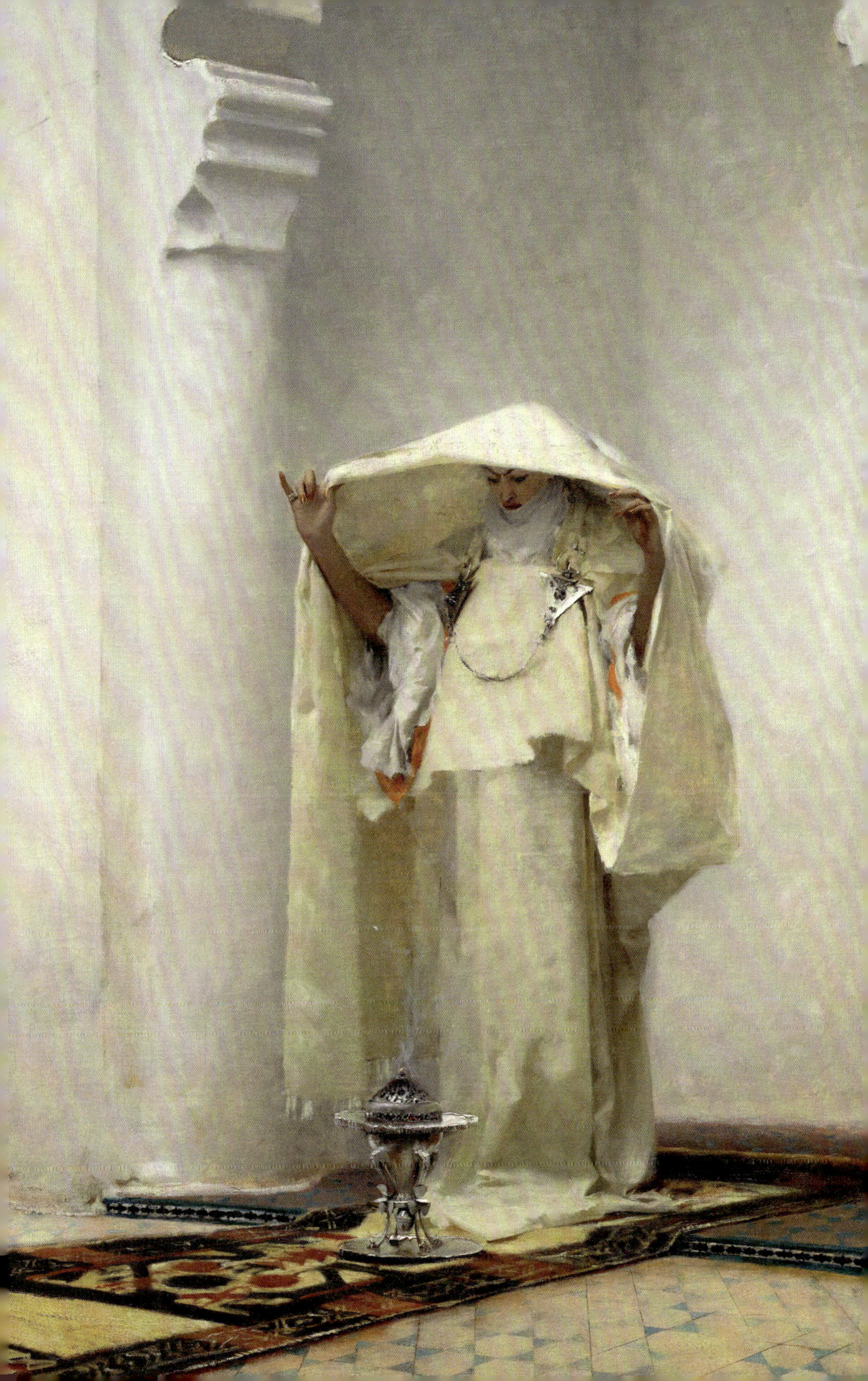

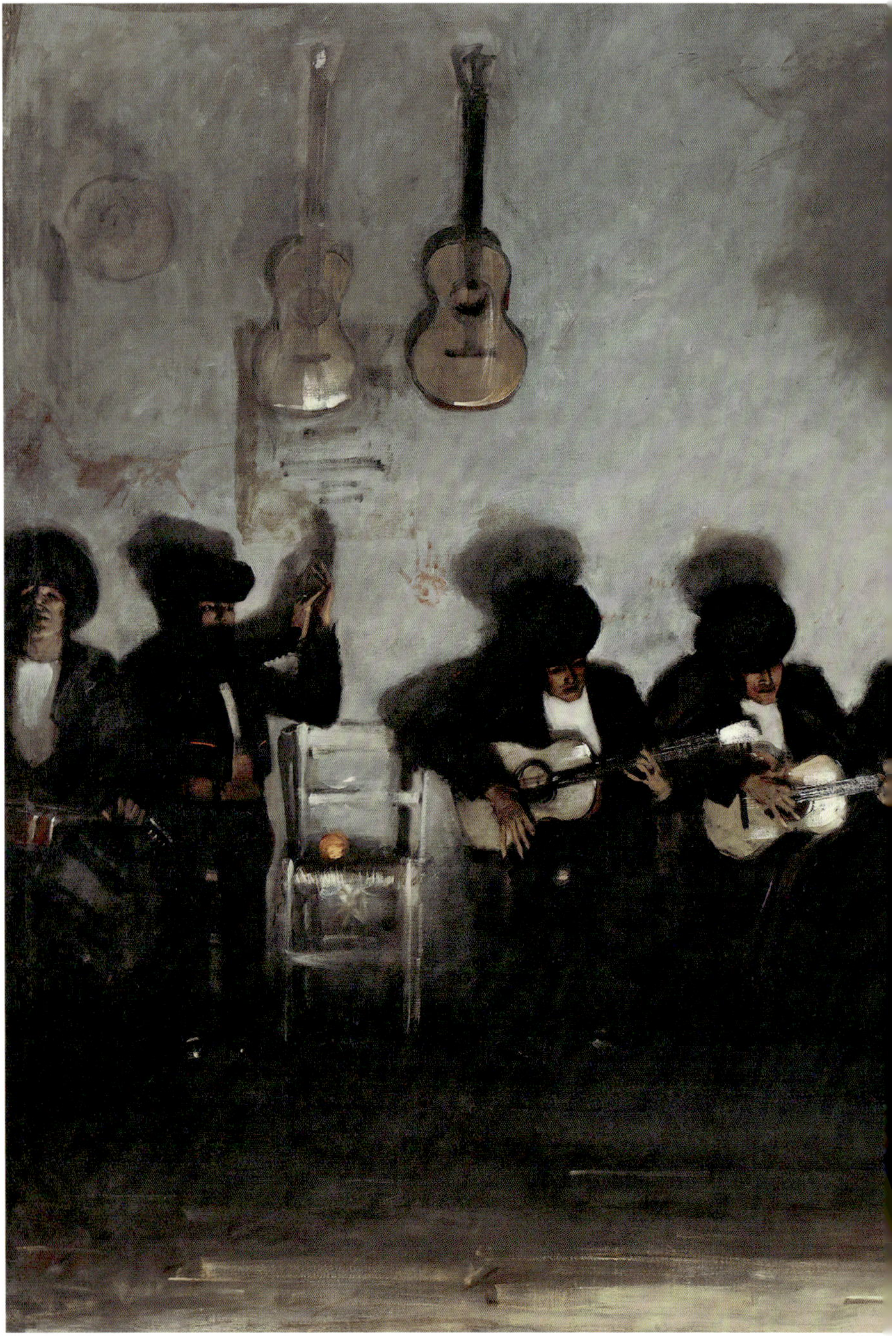

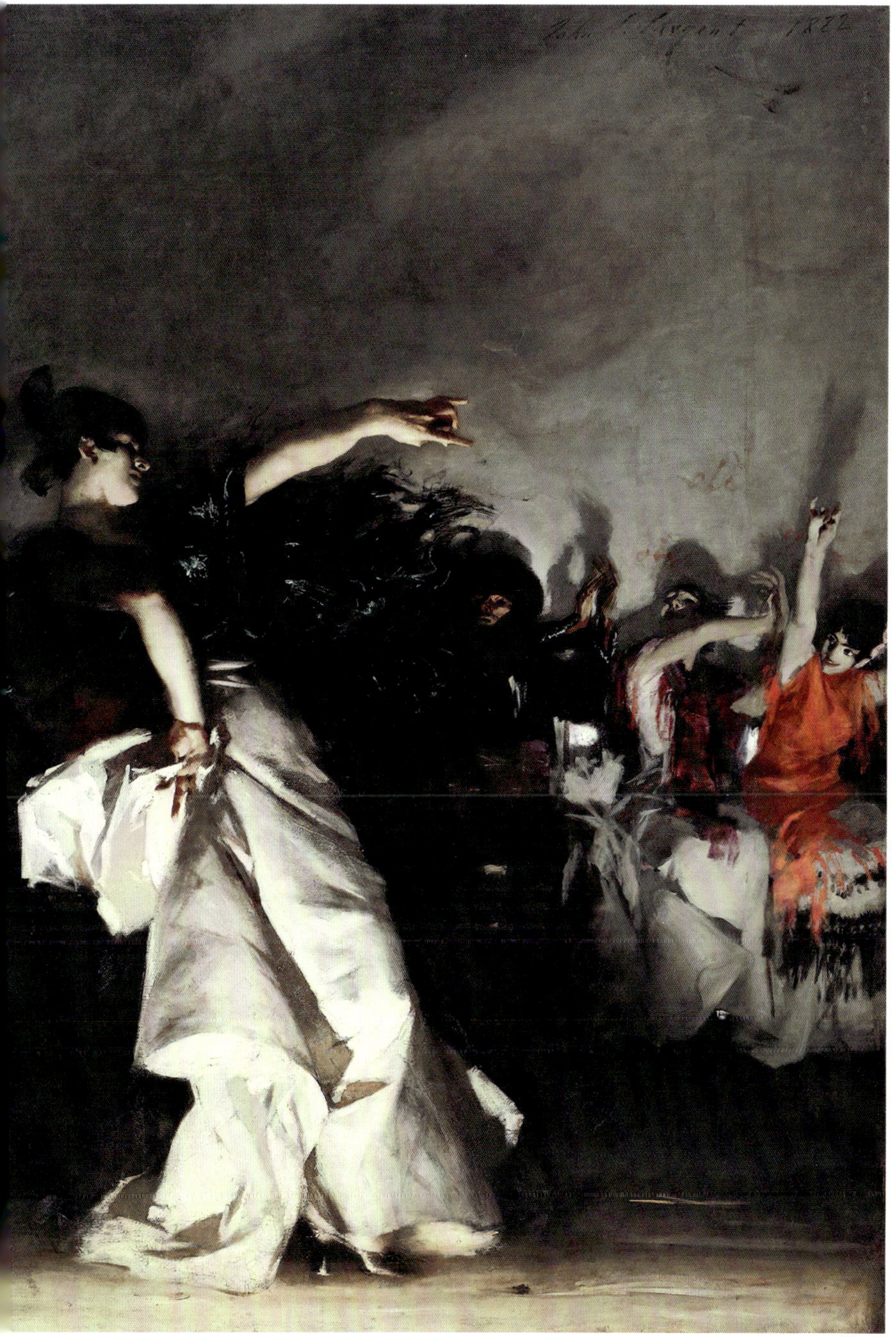

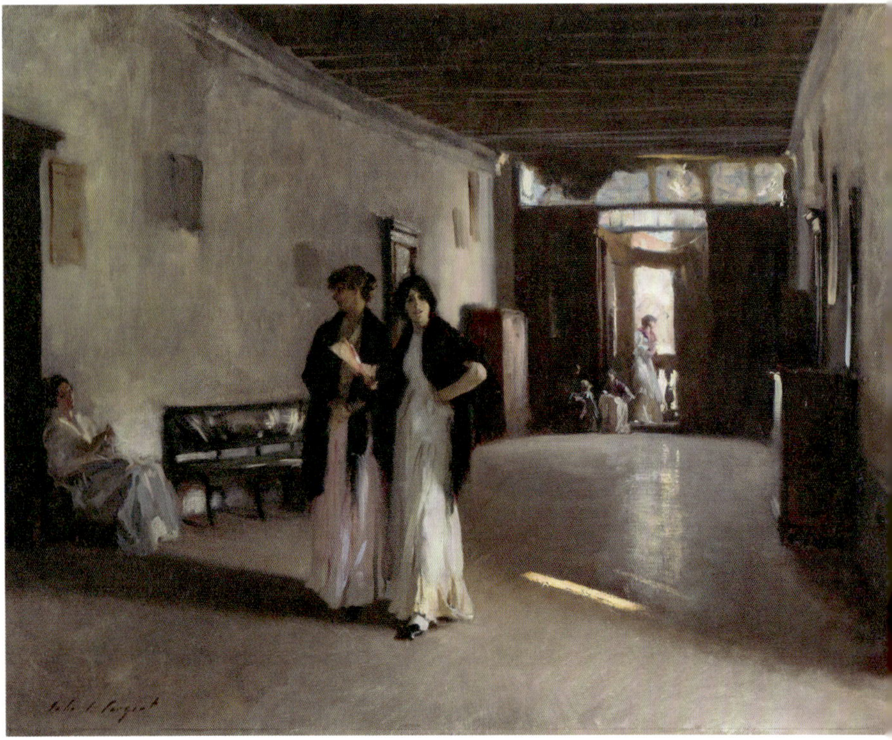

Venetian Interior c.1880–2
Oil paint on canvas
68.3 × 86.8

Pailleron Children 1881
paint on canvas
.4 × 175.3

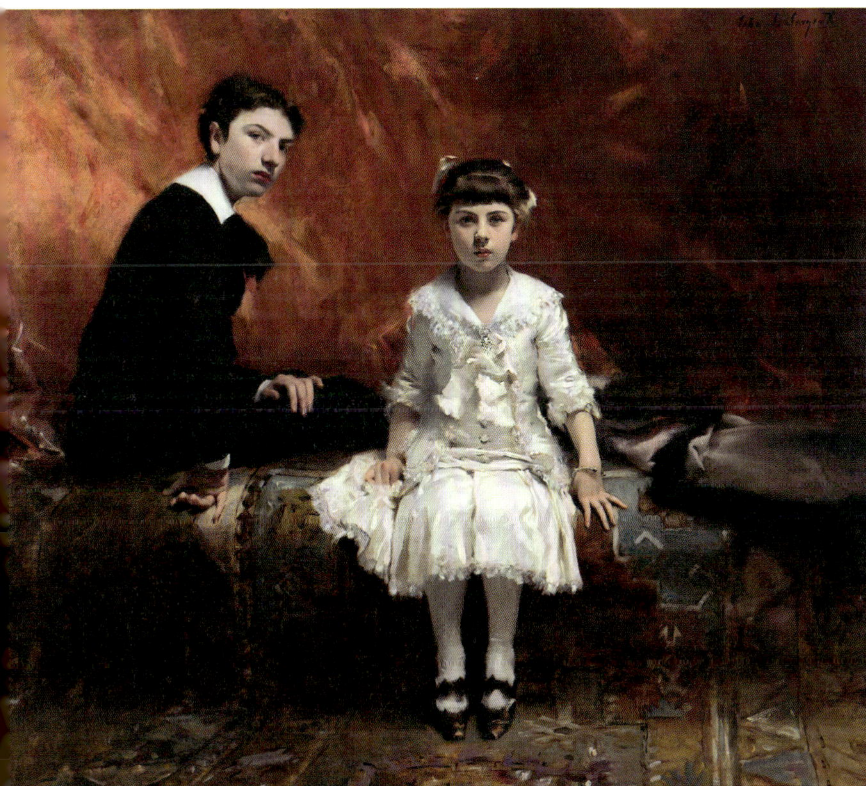

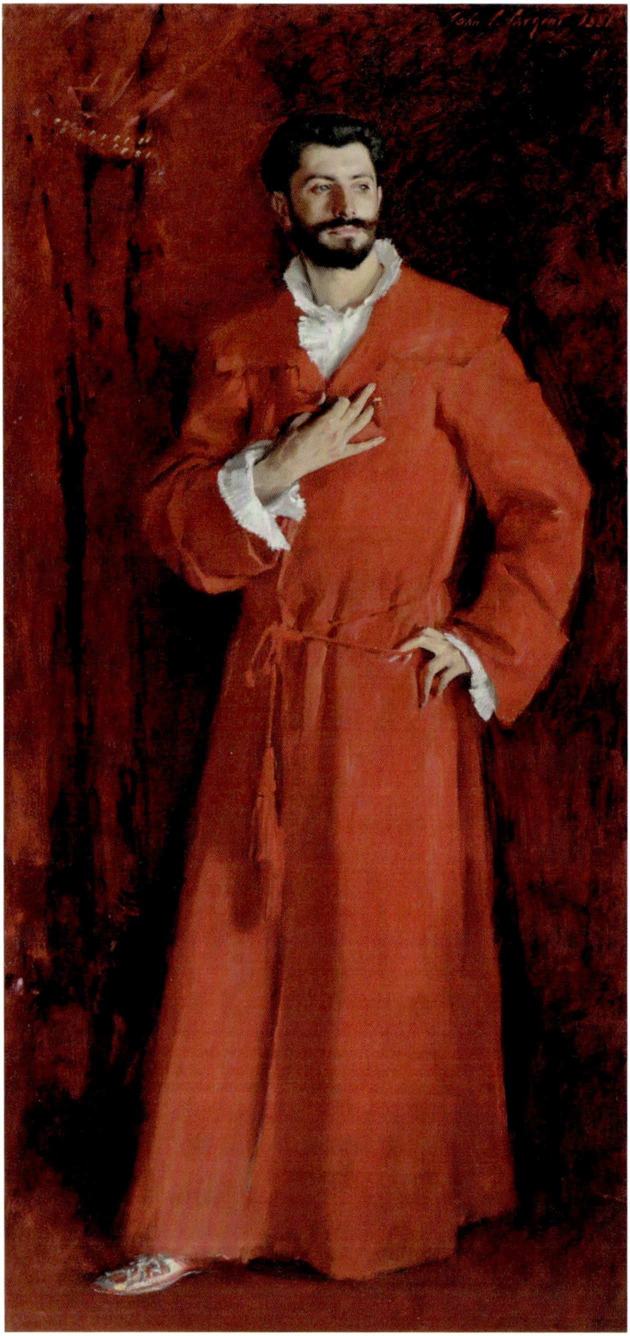

Dr Pozzi or *Dr Pozzi at Home*
1881
Oil paint on canvas
204.5 × 111.4

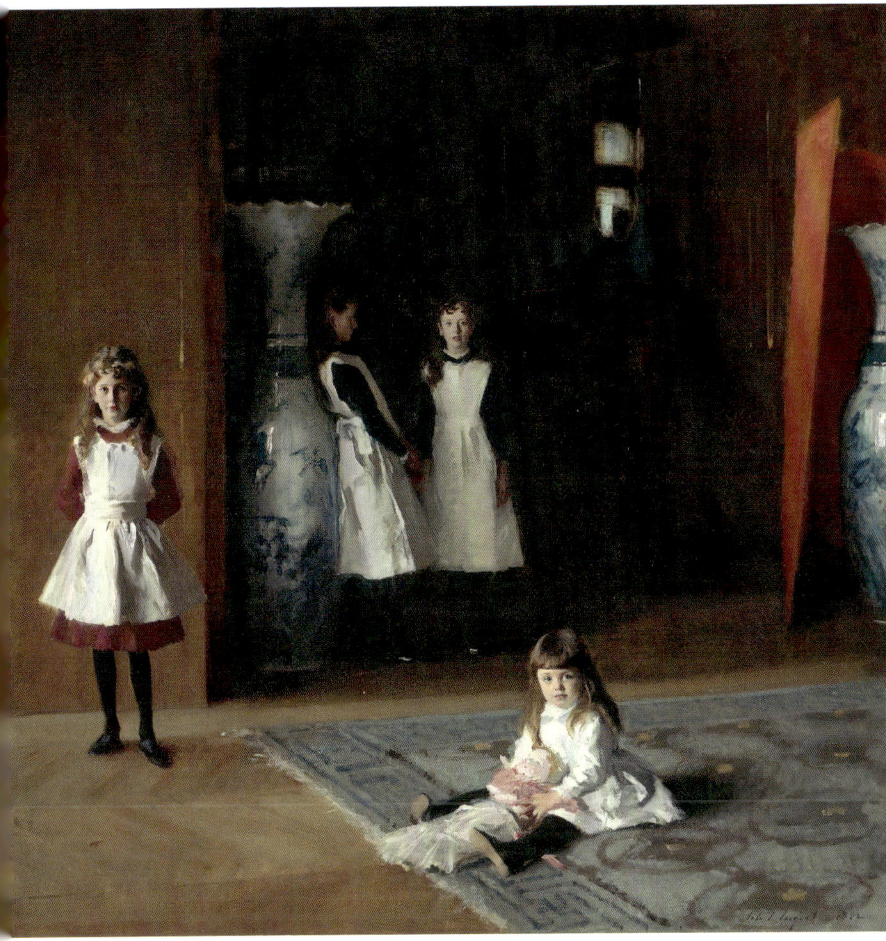

he Daughters of
dward D. Boit 1882
)il paint on canvas
21.9 × 221.6

)VERLEAF
he Misses Vickers 1884
)il paint on canvas
37.8 × 182.9

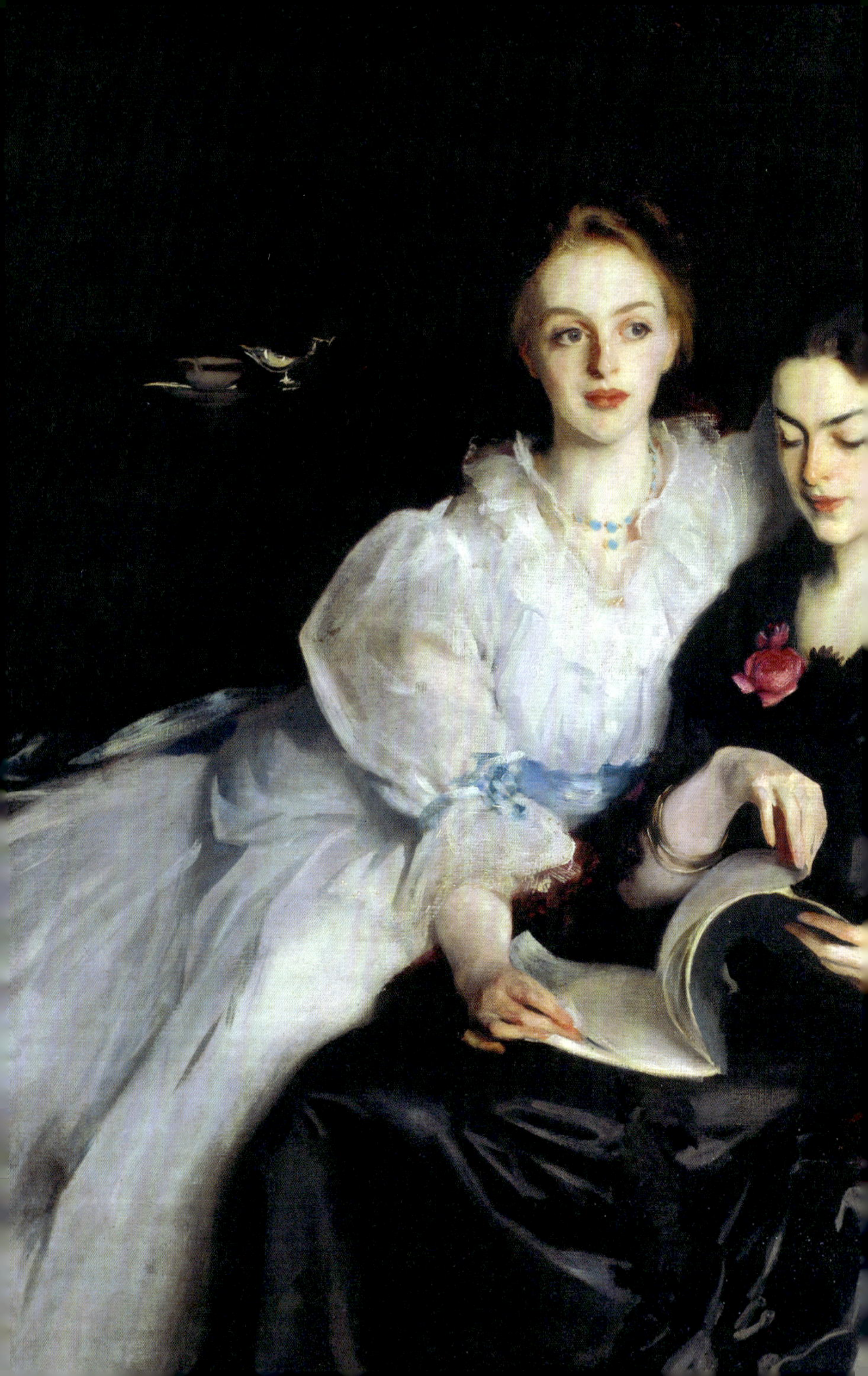

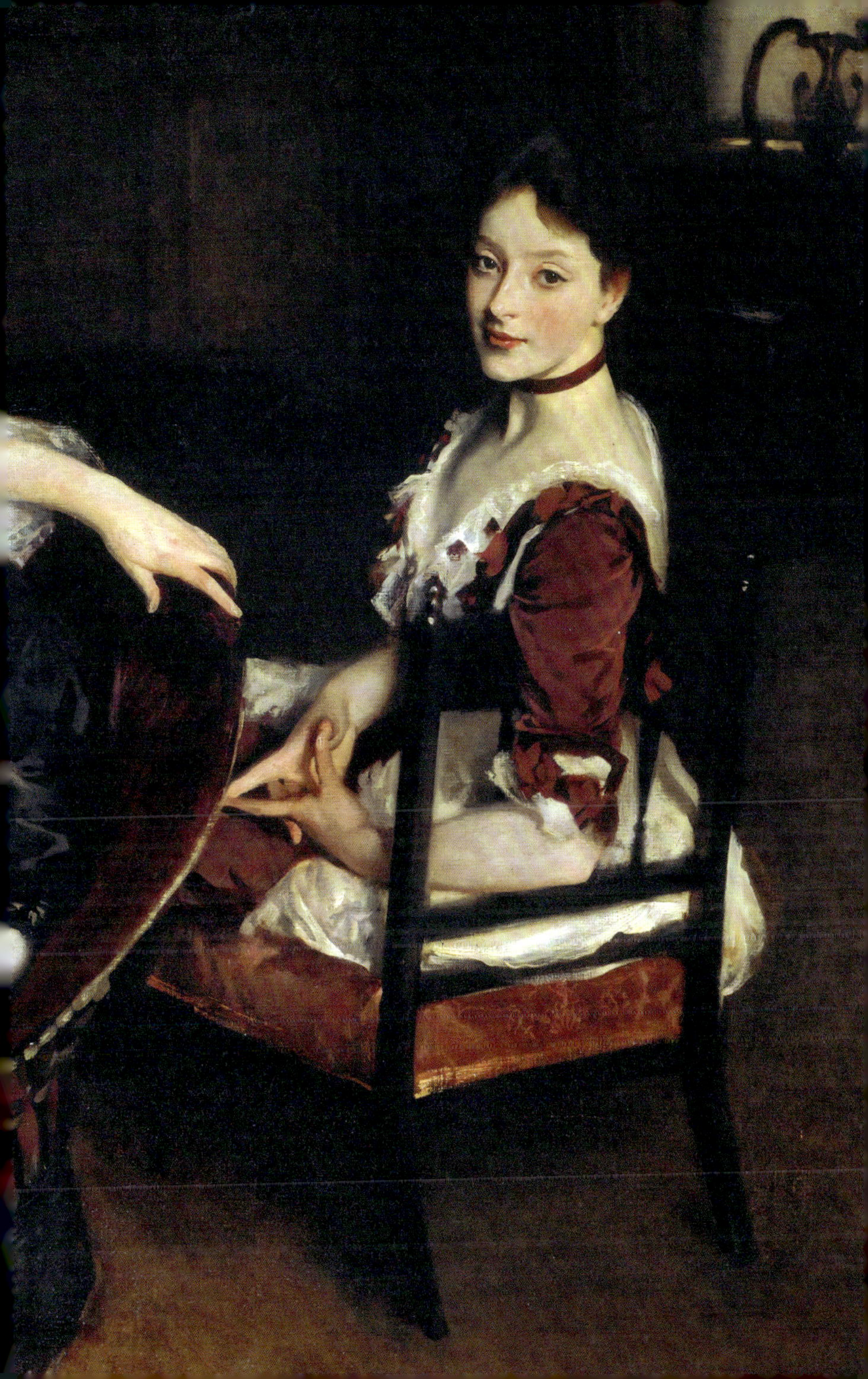

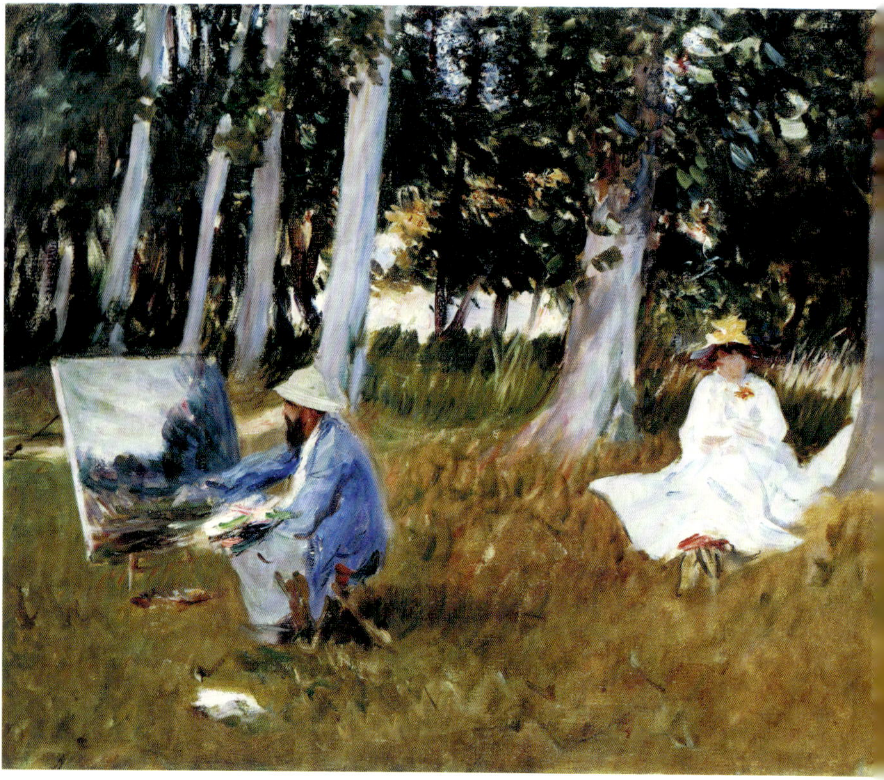

Claude Monet, painting, by the edge of a wood 1885
Oil paint on canvas
54 × 64.8

: *Familiale* or *The Birthday*
ty ?c.1885
paint on canvas
× 73.7

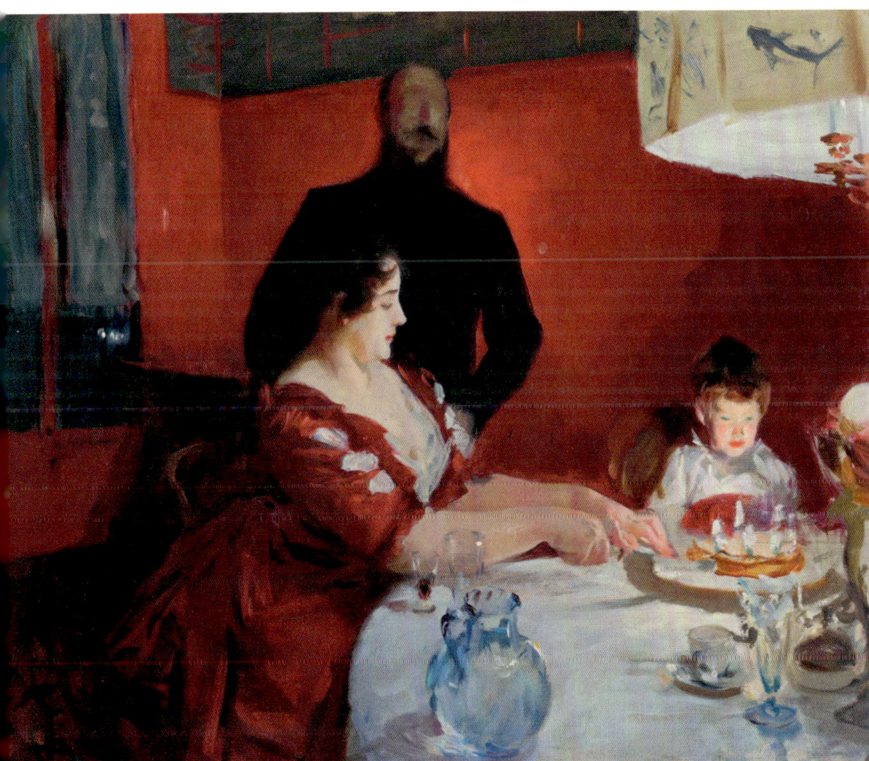

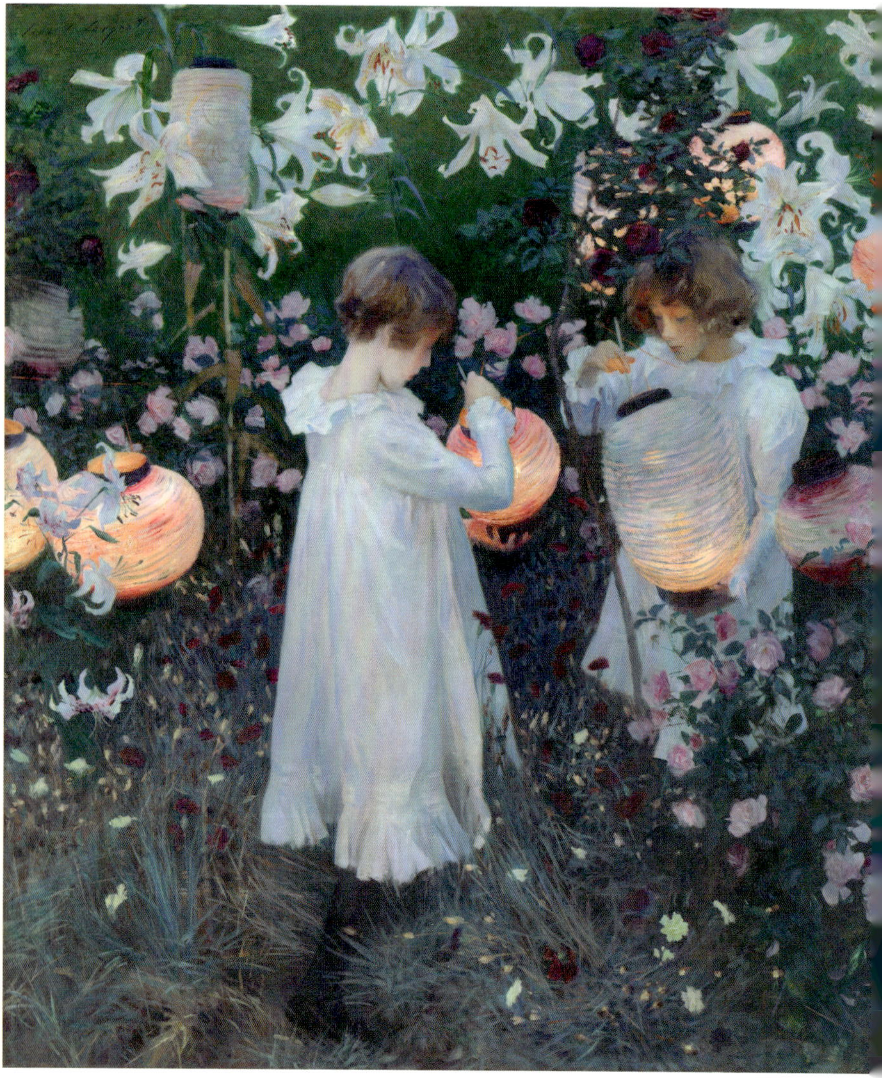

Carnation, Lily, Lily, Rose
1885–6
Oil paint on canvas
174 × 153.7

Ruth Sears Bacon 1887
Oil paint on canvas
123.8 × 92.1

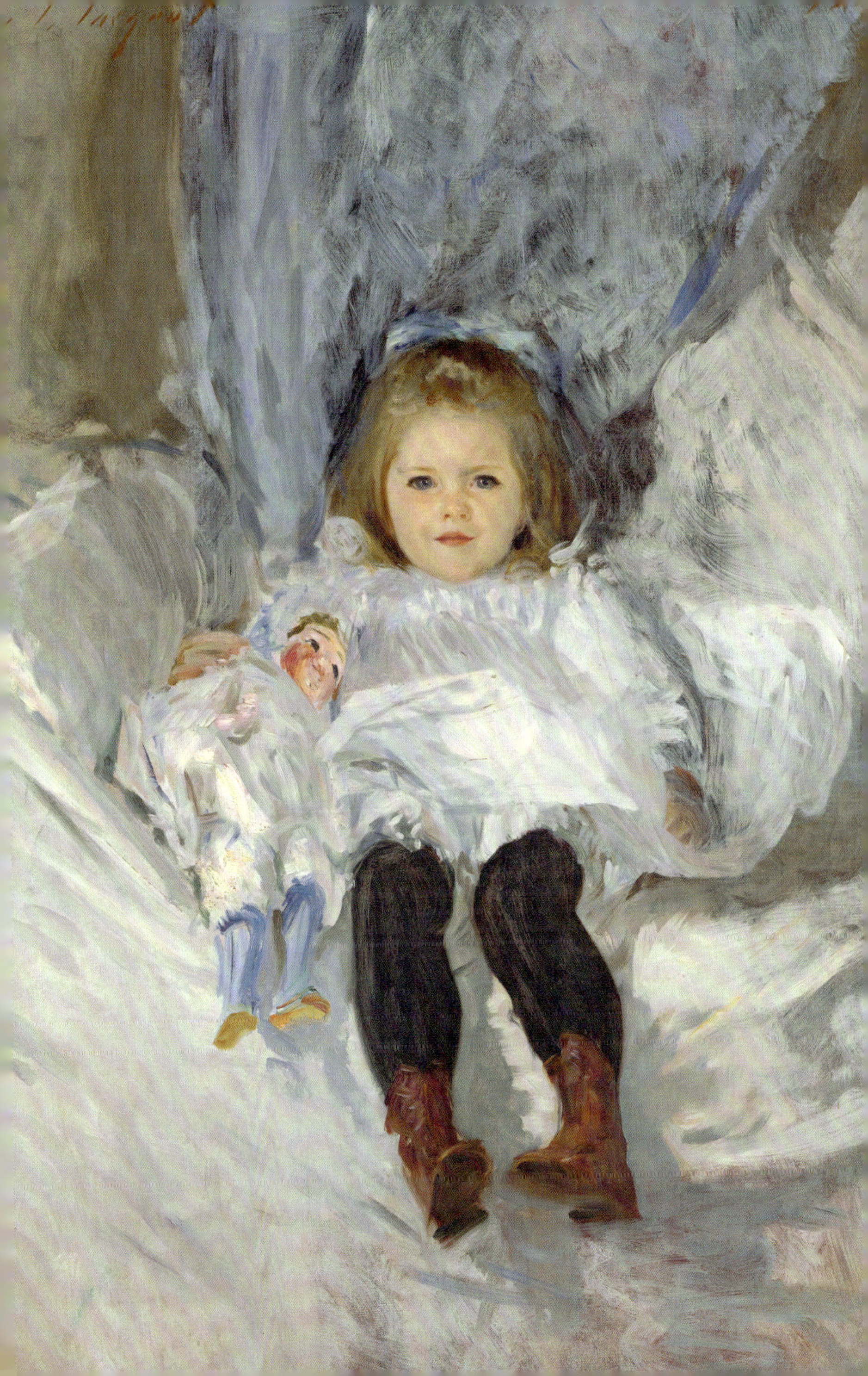

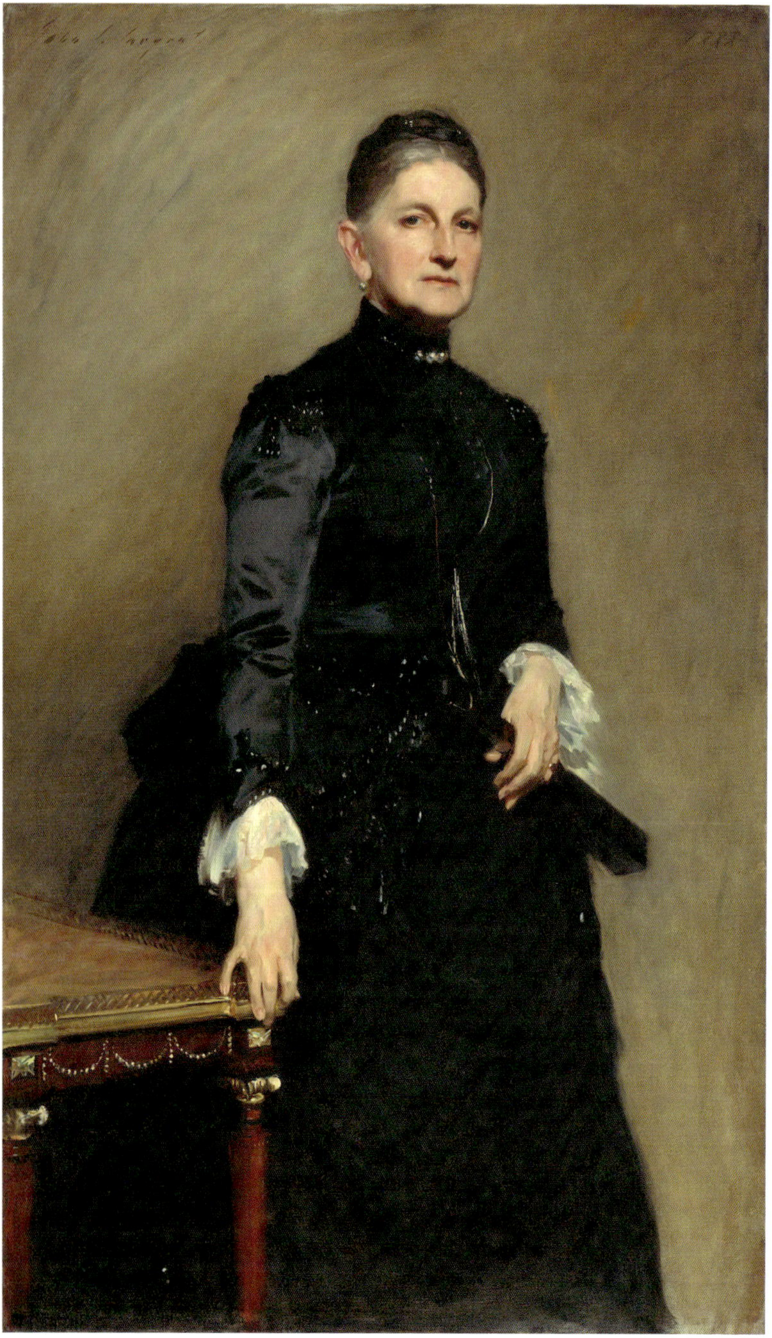

rs Adrian Iselin 1888
l paint on canvas
3.7 × 93

en Terry as Lady Macbeth
89
l paint on canvas
1 × 114.3

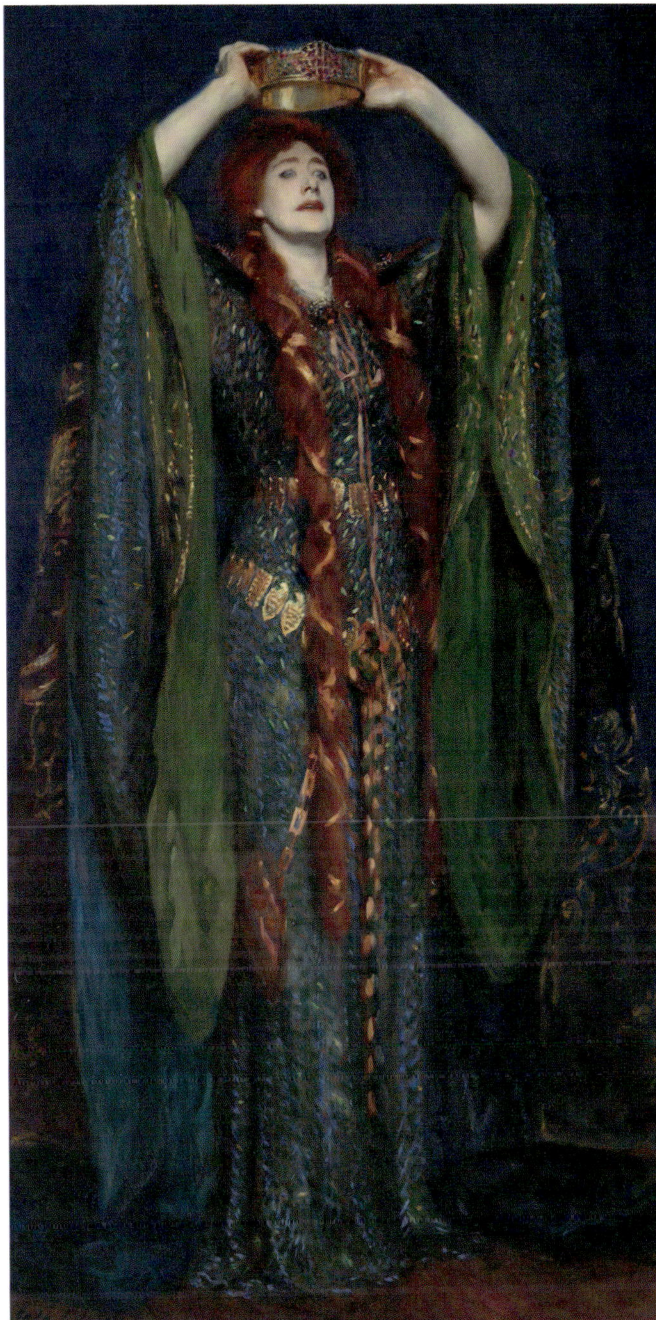

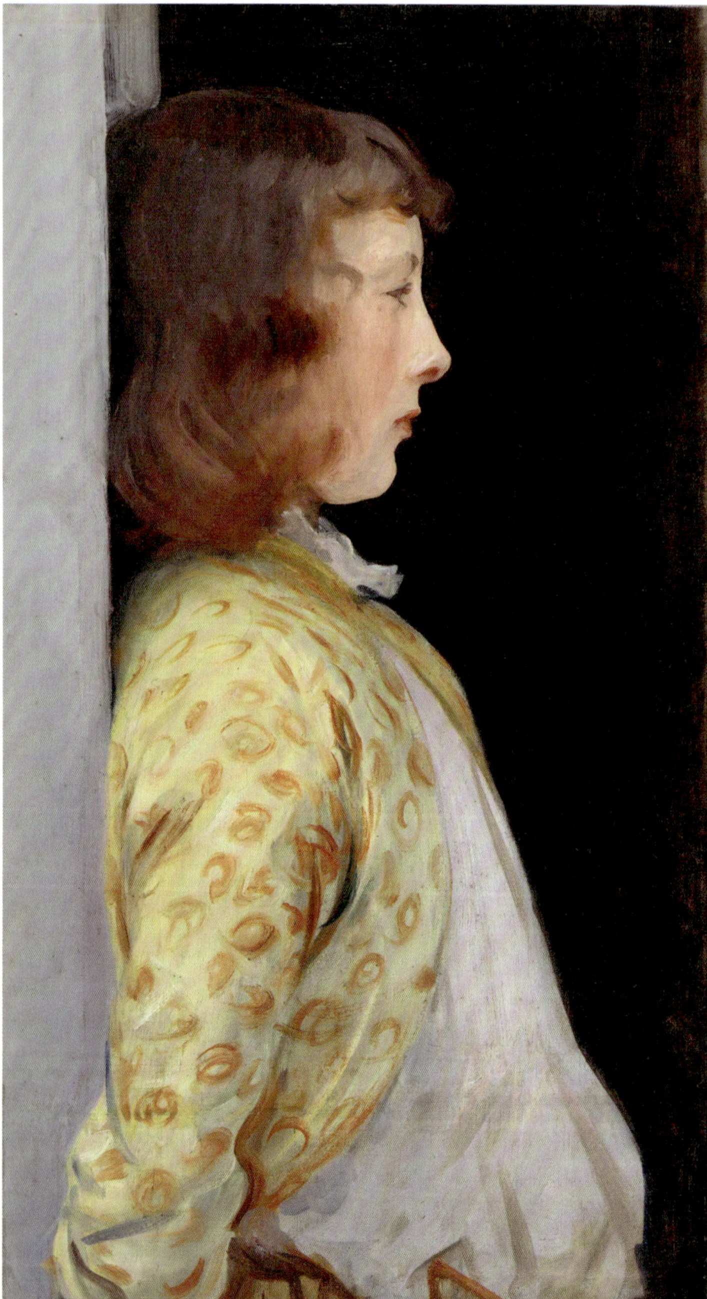

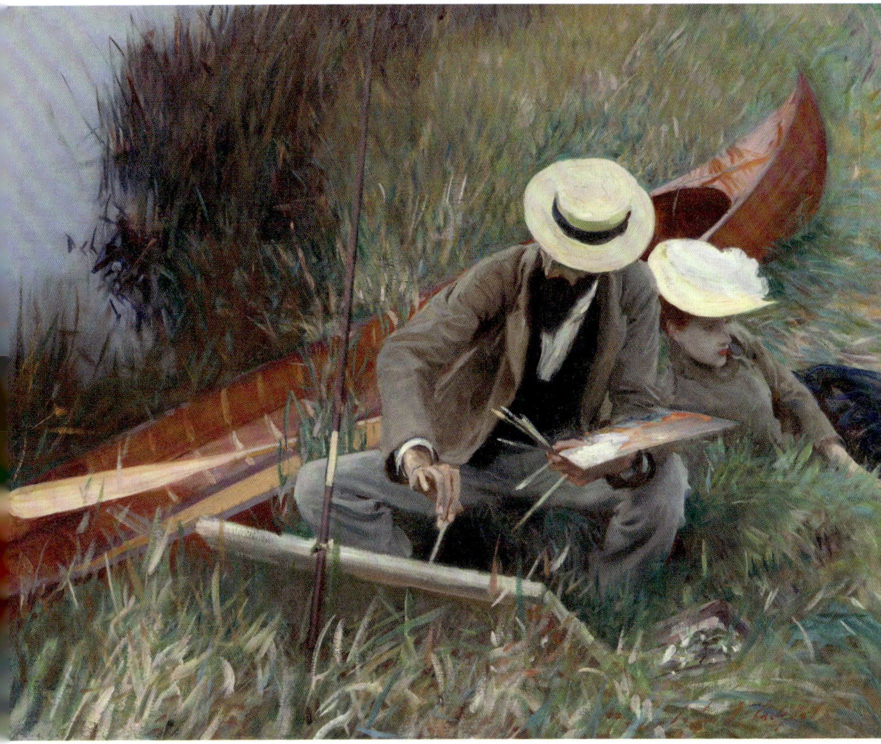

orothy Barnard 1889
il paint on canvas
0.5 × 39.4

aul Helleu Sketching with
is Wife or An Out-of-Doors
udy 1889
il paint on canvas
6.3 × 81.5

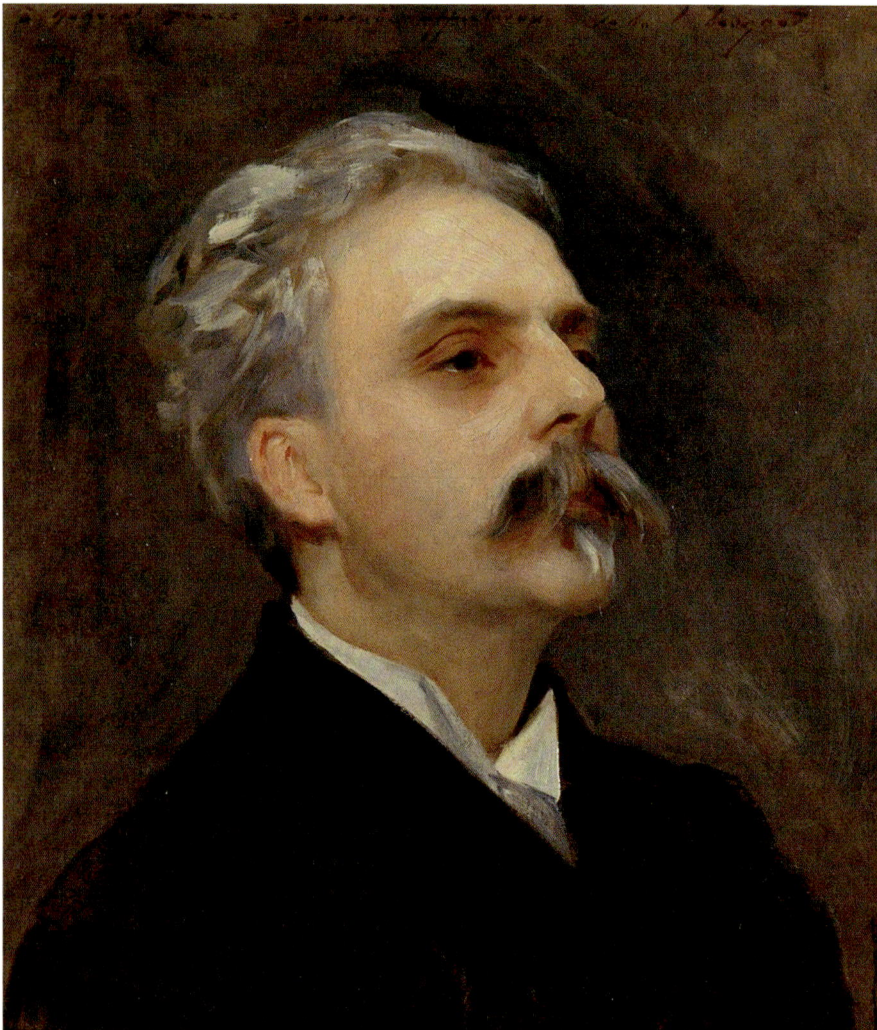

Gabriel Fauré c.1889
Oil paint on canvas
61 × 54.6

Elsie Palmer 1889–90
Oil paint on canvas
190.5 × 114.3

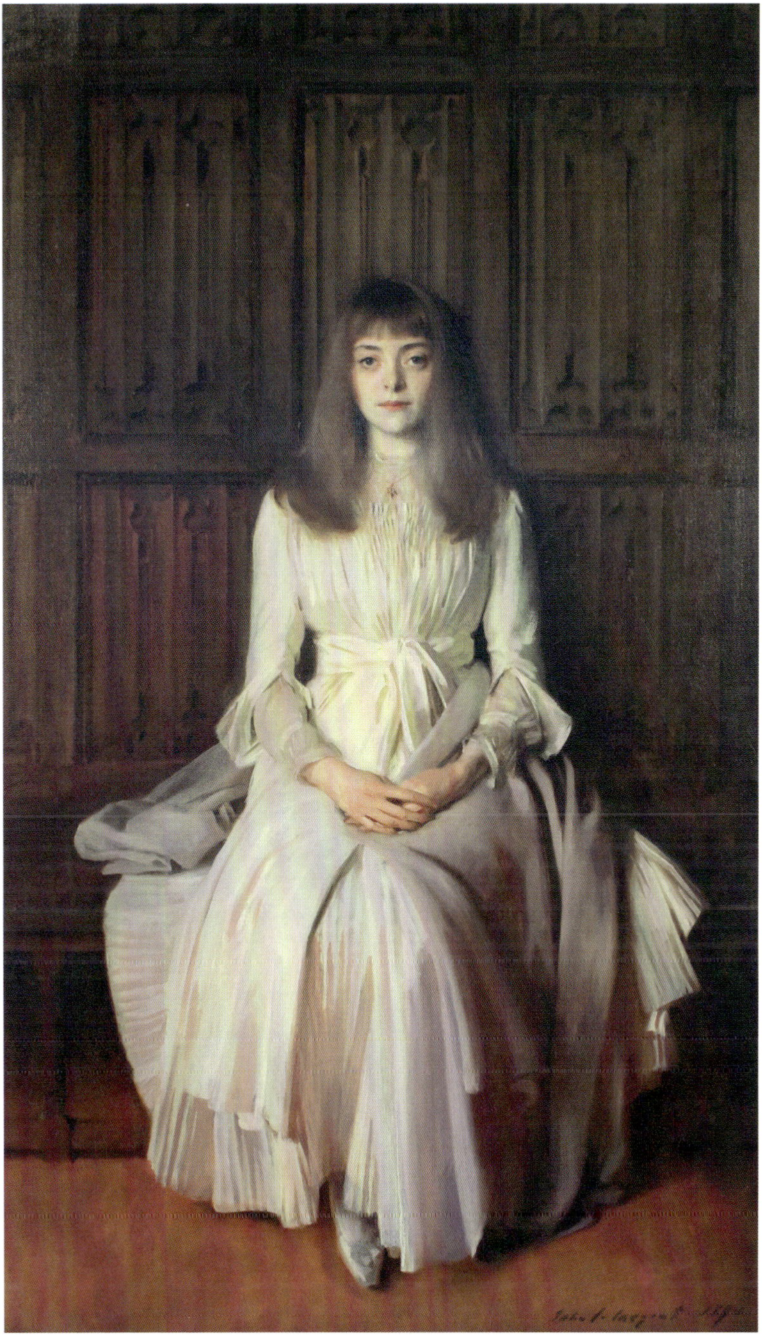

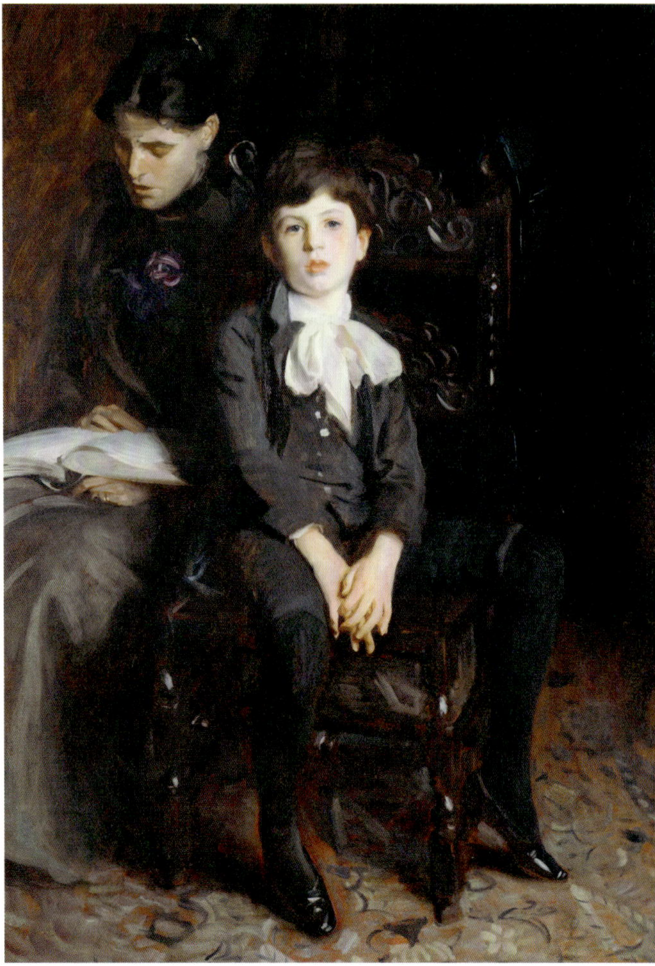

Homer Saint-Gaudens and his Mother 1890
Oil paint on canvas
151.8 × 142.2

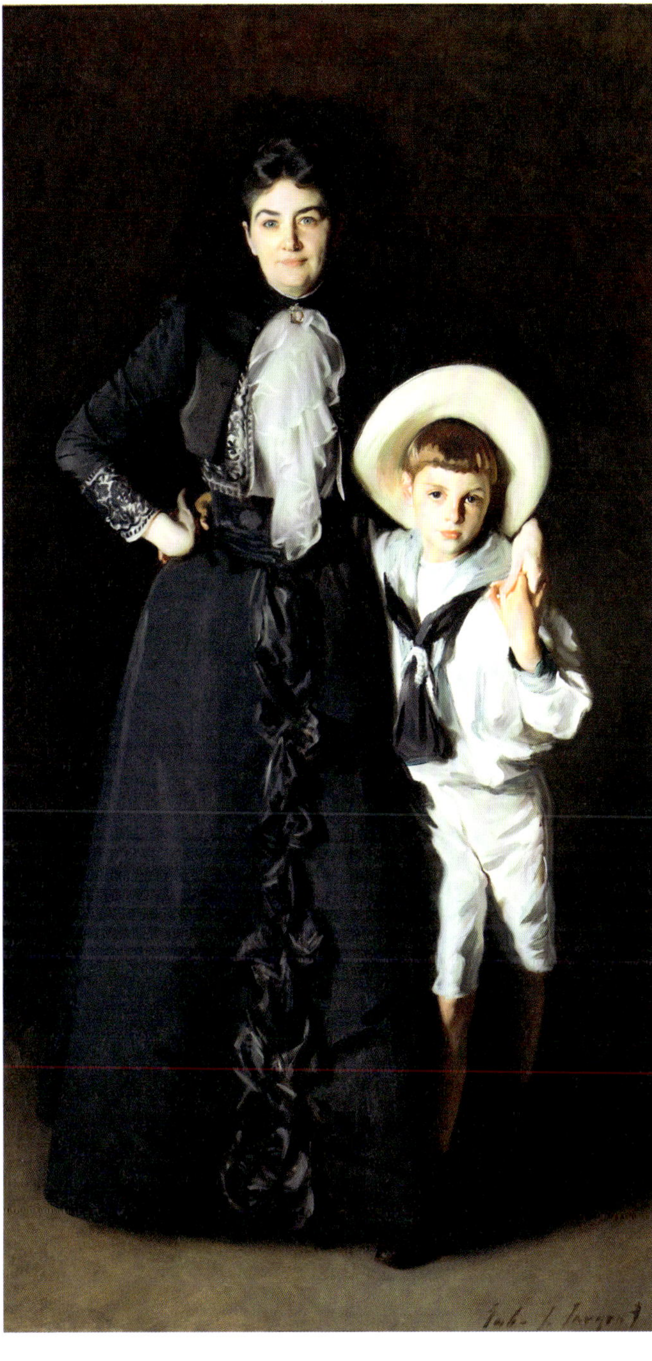

's Edward Davis and
' Son, Livingston 1890
l paint on canvas
8.8 × 122.6

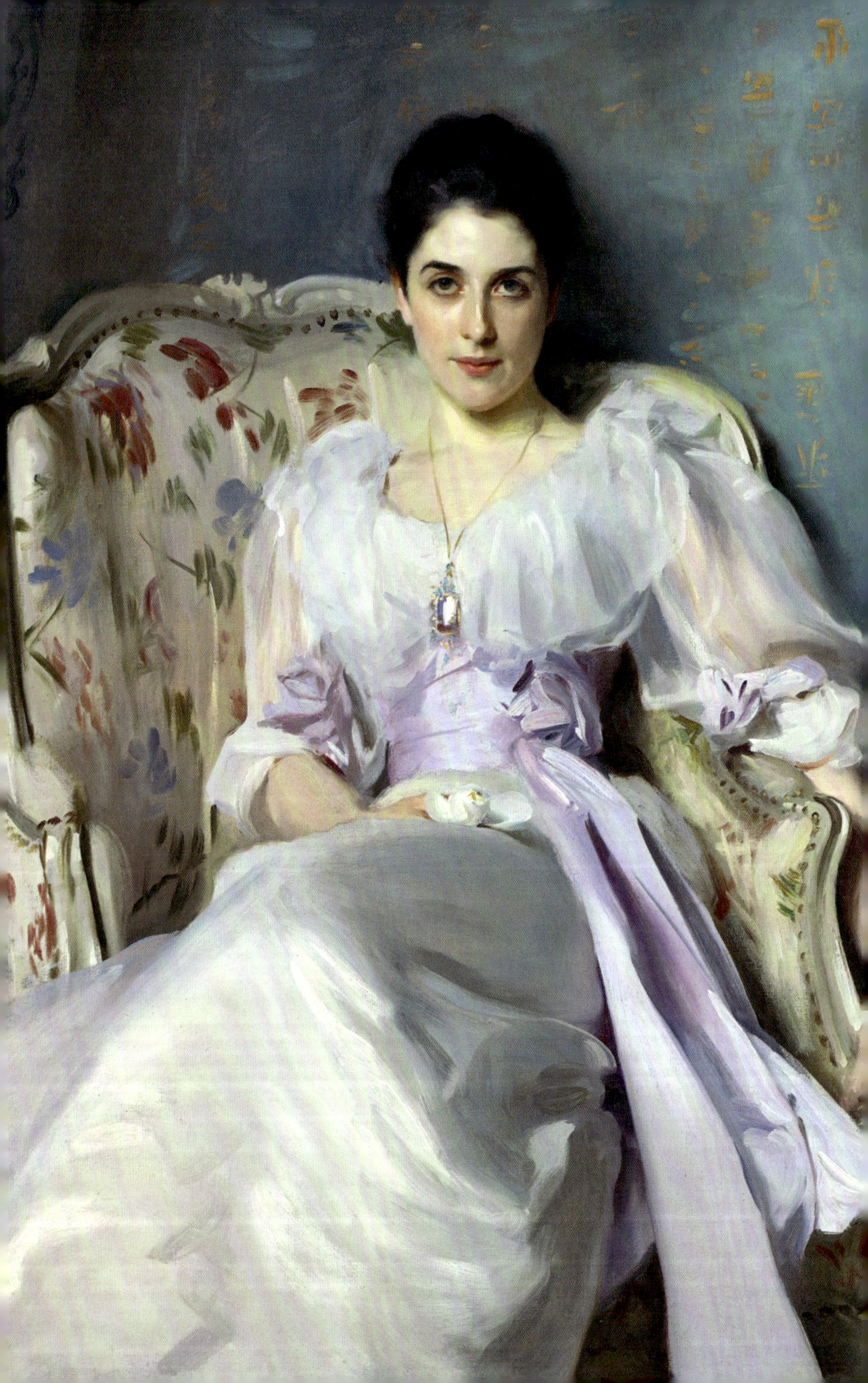

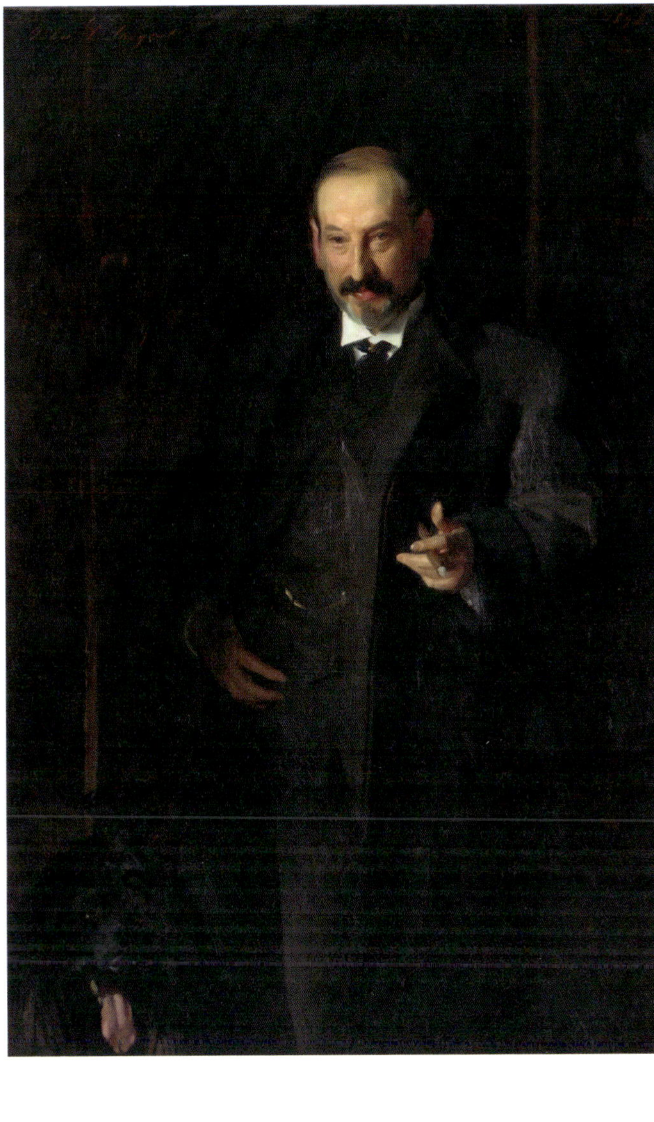

Lady Agnew of Lochnaw 1892
Oil paint on canvas
125.7 × 100.3

Asher Wertheimer 1897–8
Oil paint on canvas
147.5 × 98

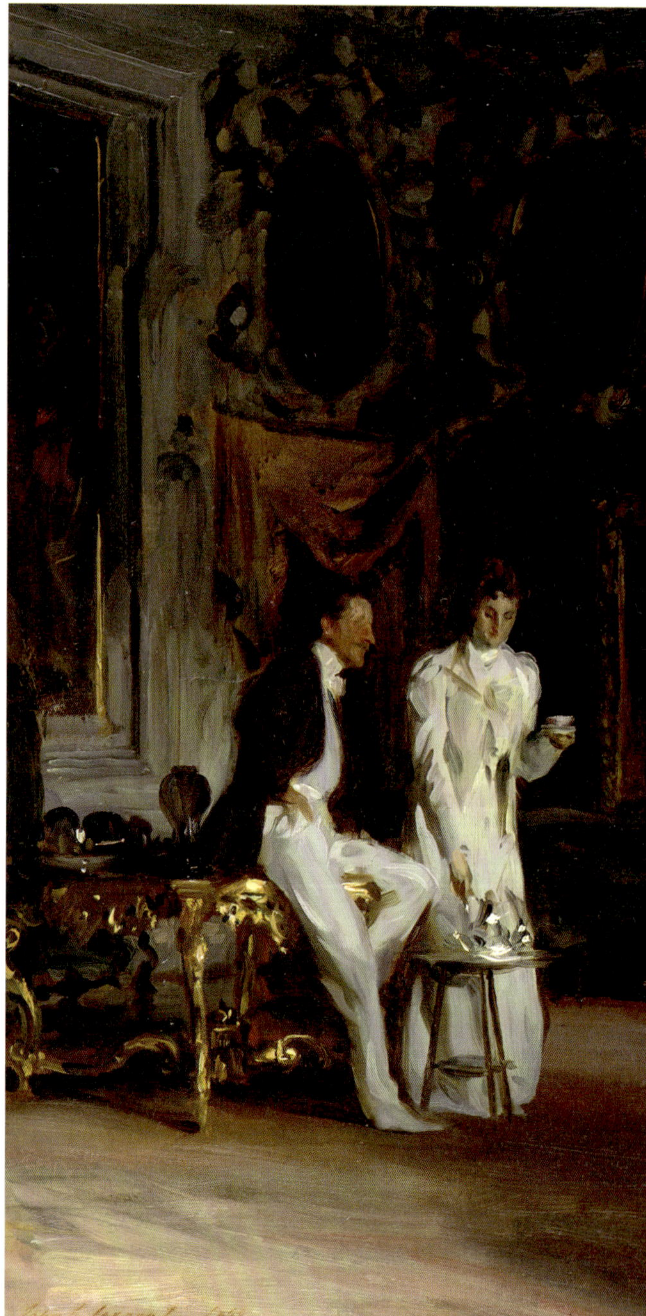

An Interior in Venice 1898
Oil paint on canvas
66 × 83.5

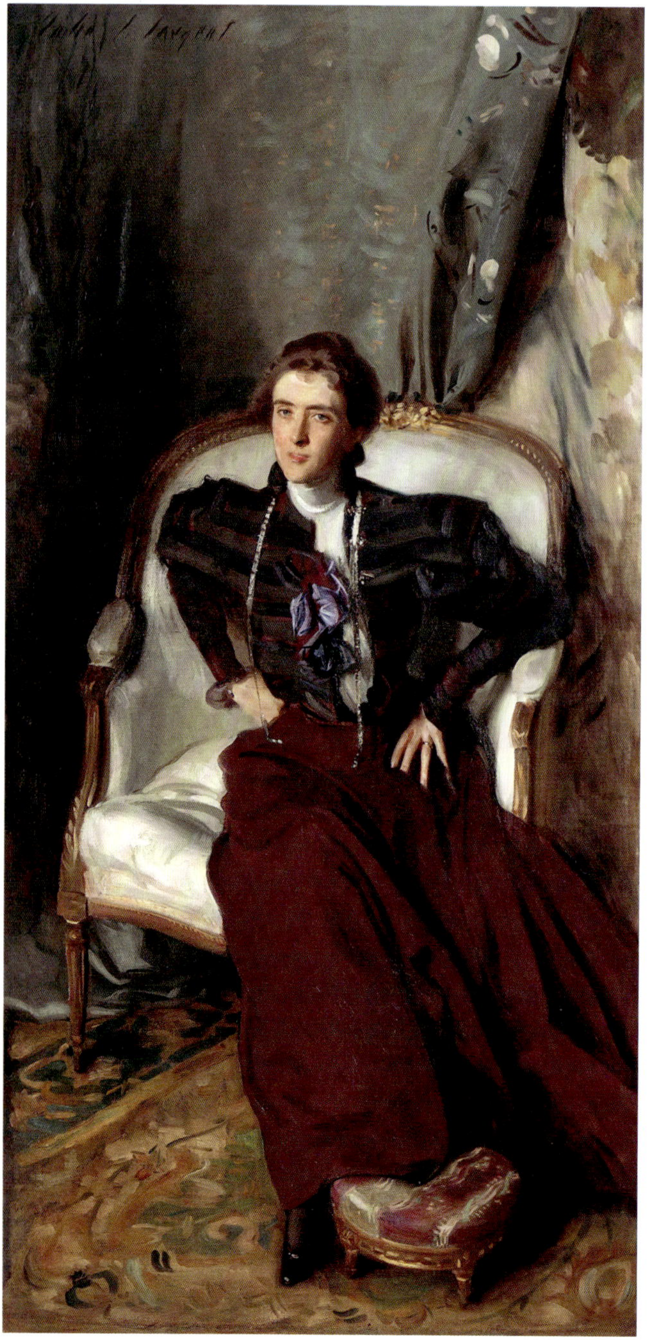

Mrs Charles Thursby c.1898
Oil paint on canvas
198.1 × 101

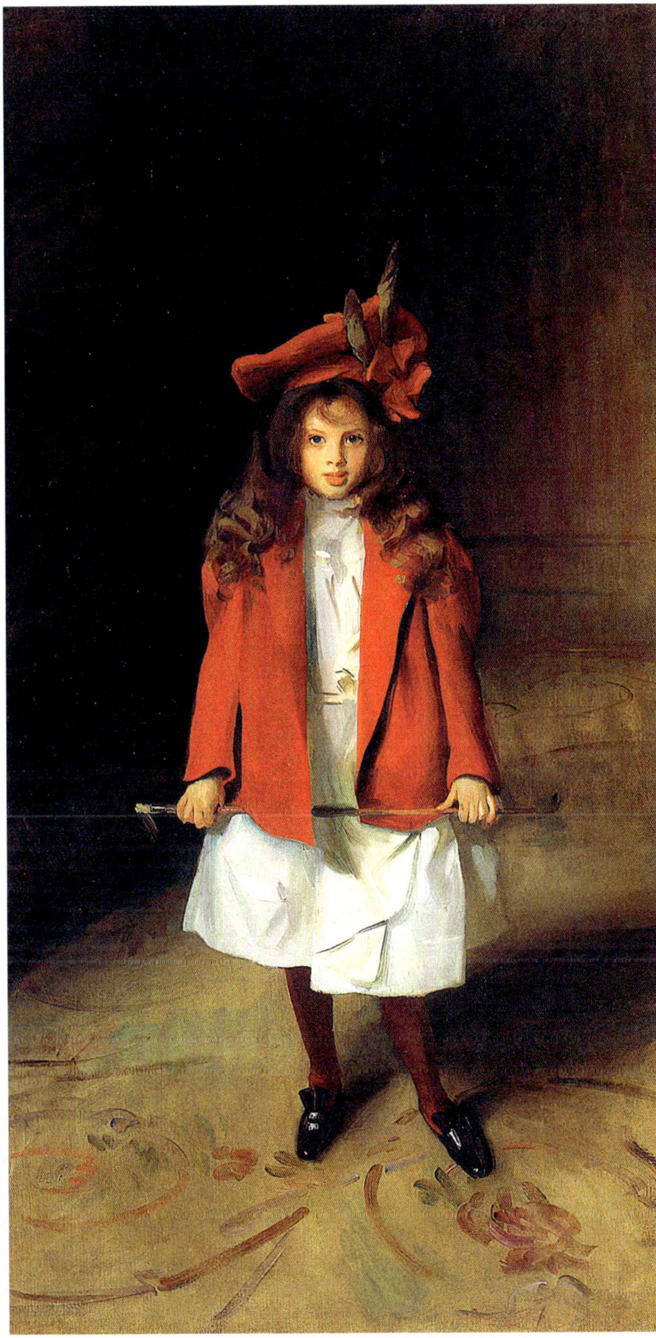

e Honourable Victoria
nley 1899
l paint on canvas
5.8 × 105.4

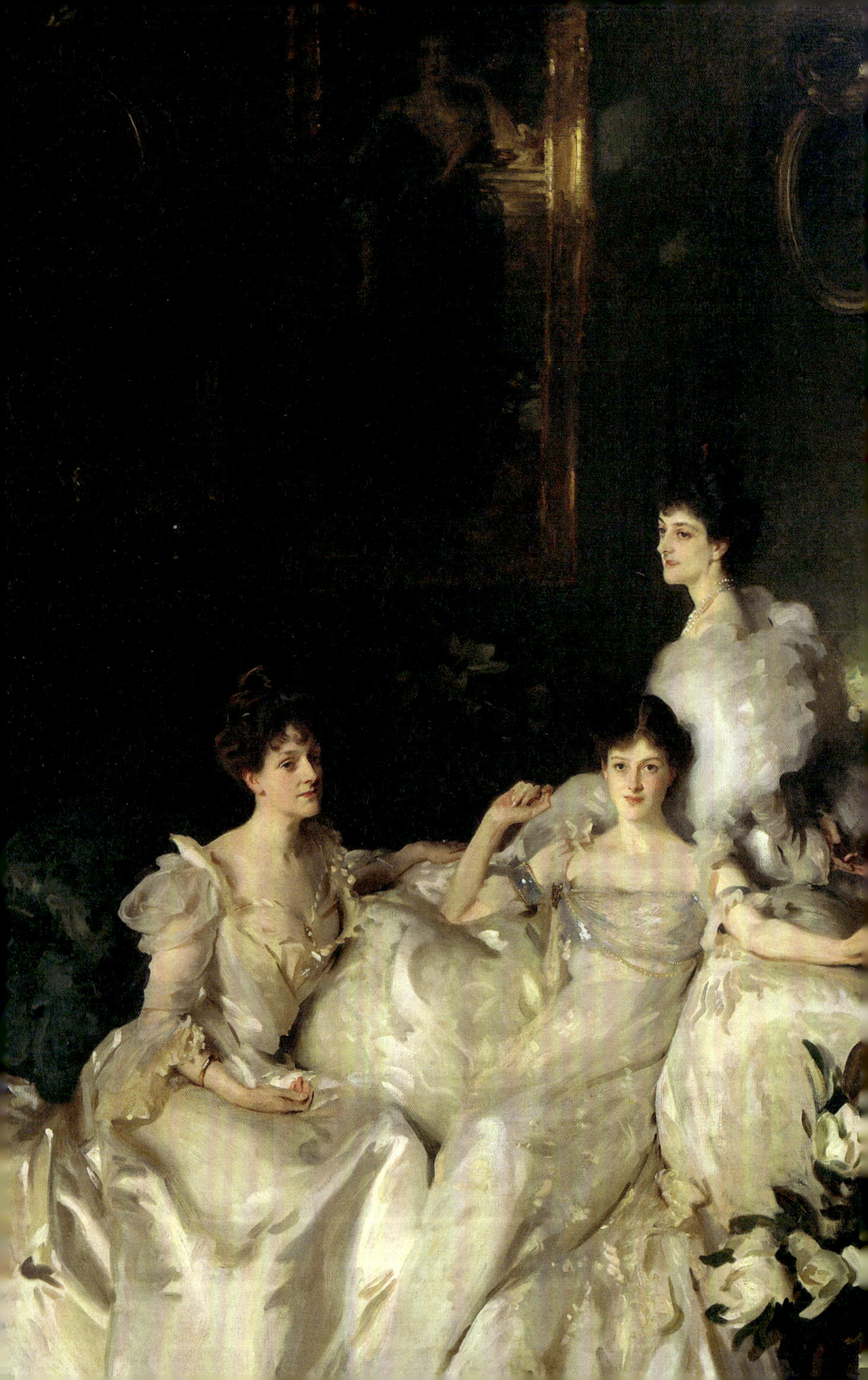

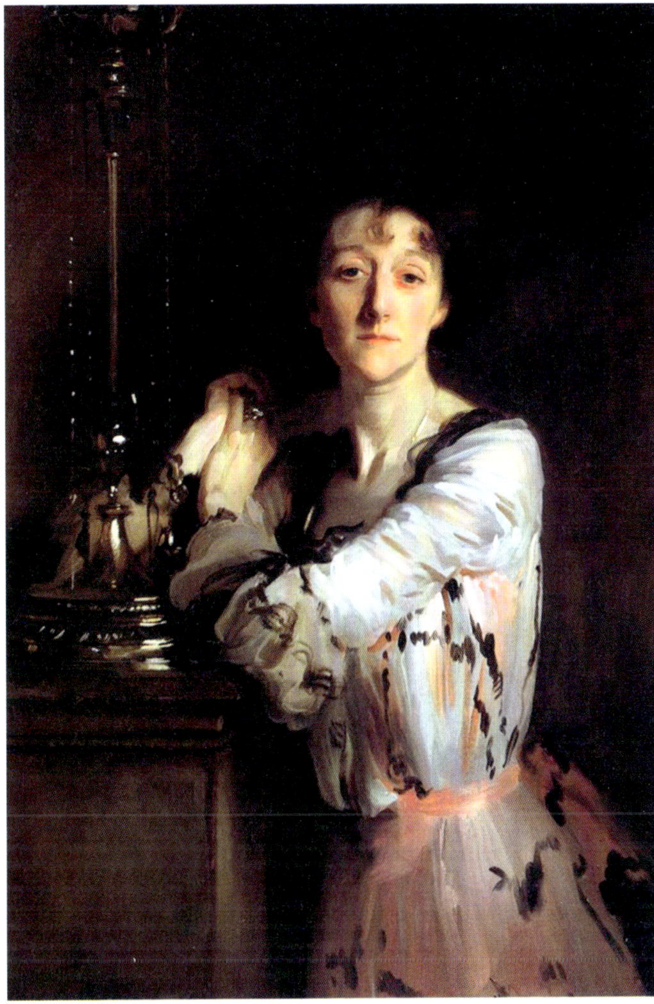

Lady Elcho, Mrs Adeane and Mrs Tennant or The Wyndham Sisters 1899
Oil paint on canvas
292.1 × 213.7

The Honourable Mrs Charles Russell 1900
Oil paint on canvas
104.8 × 73.7

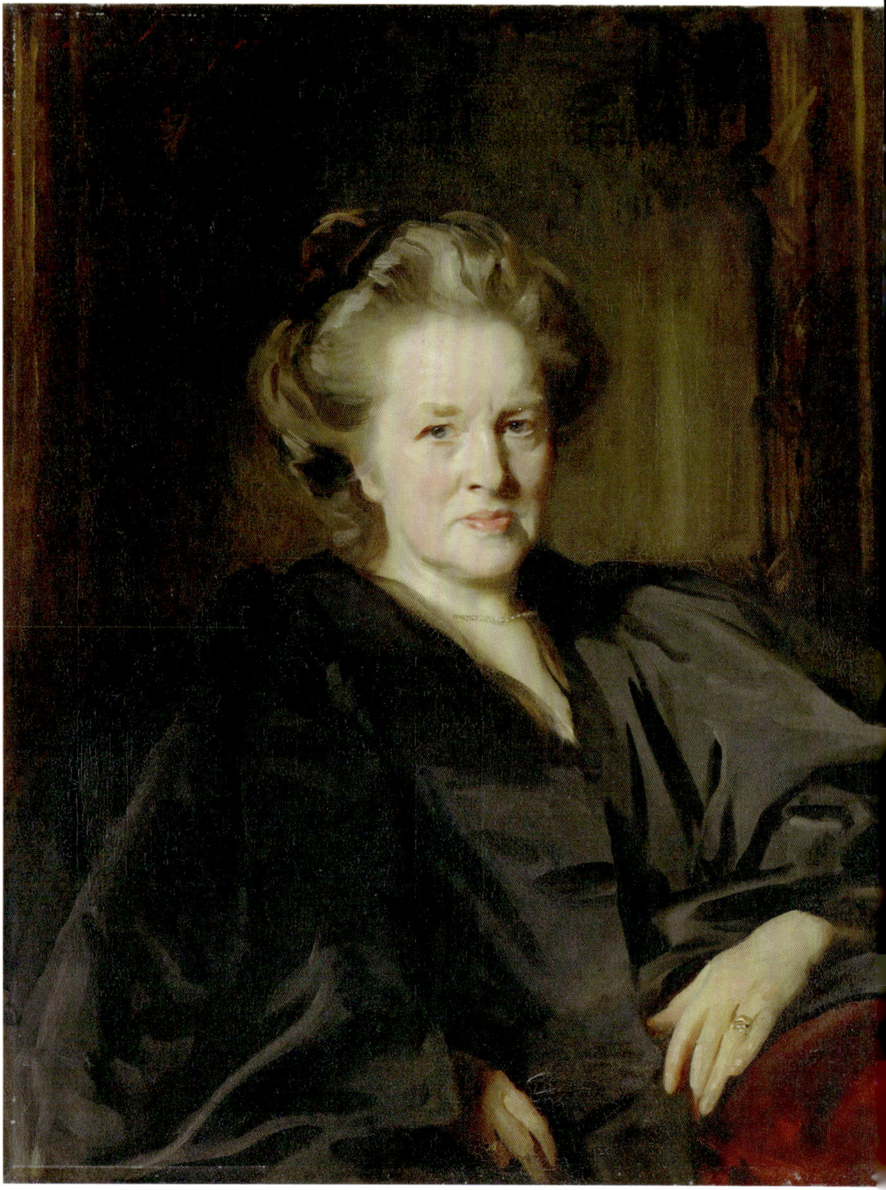

Elizabeth Garrett Anderson 1900
Oil paint on canvas
83.8 × 66

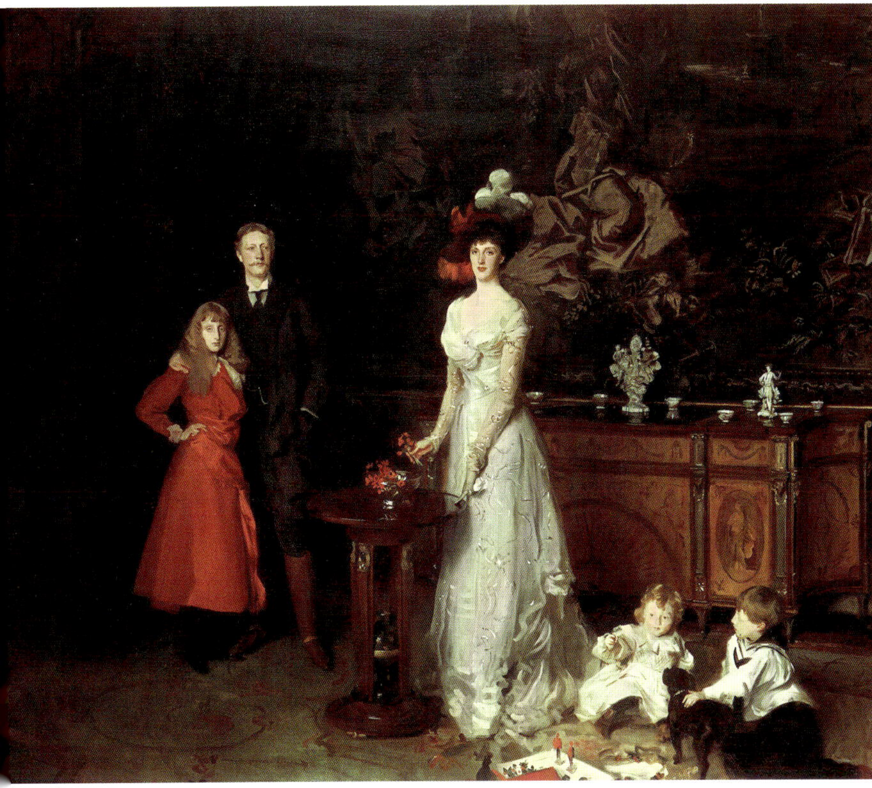

· George Sitwell, Lady Ida
:well and Family 1900
.l paint on canvas
0.2 × 193

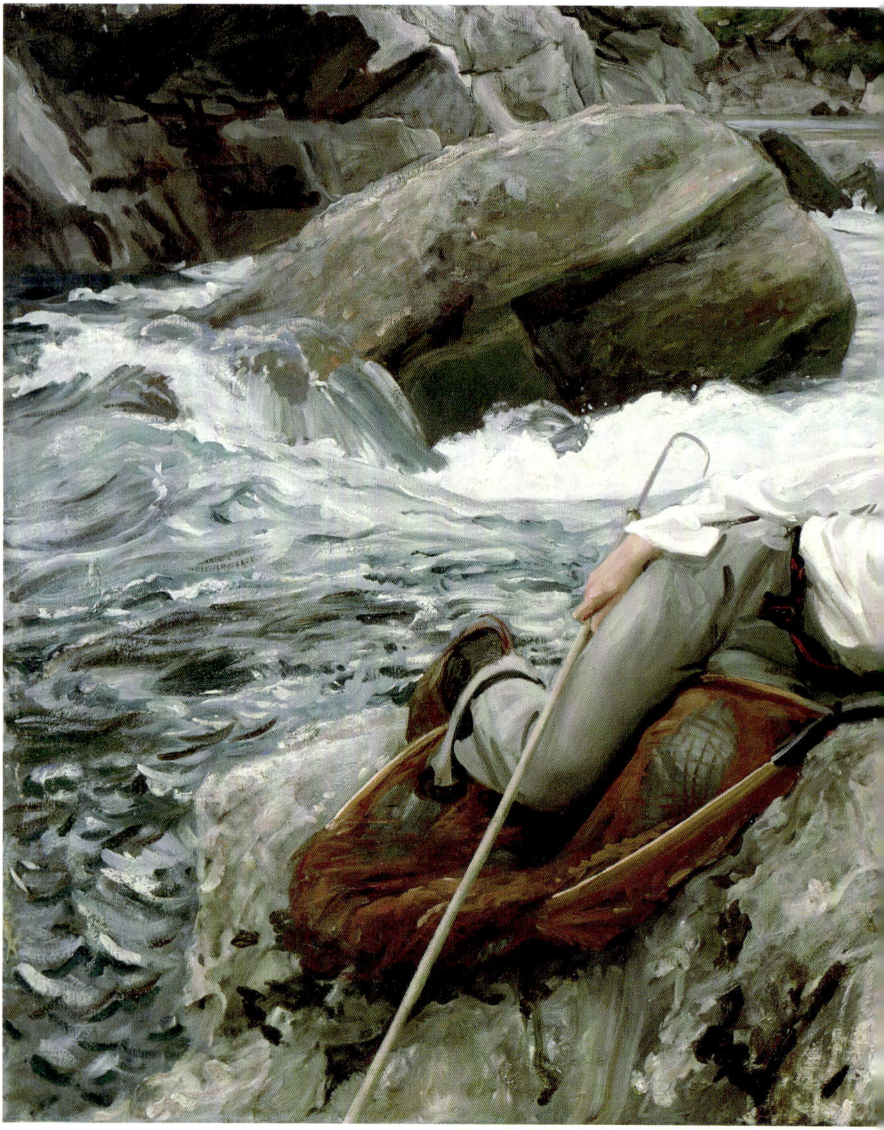

On his Holidays, Norway 1901
Oil paint on canvas
137 × 244

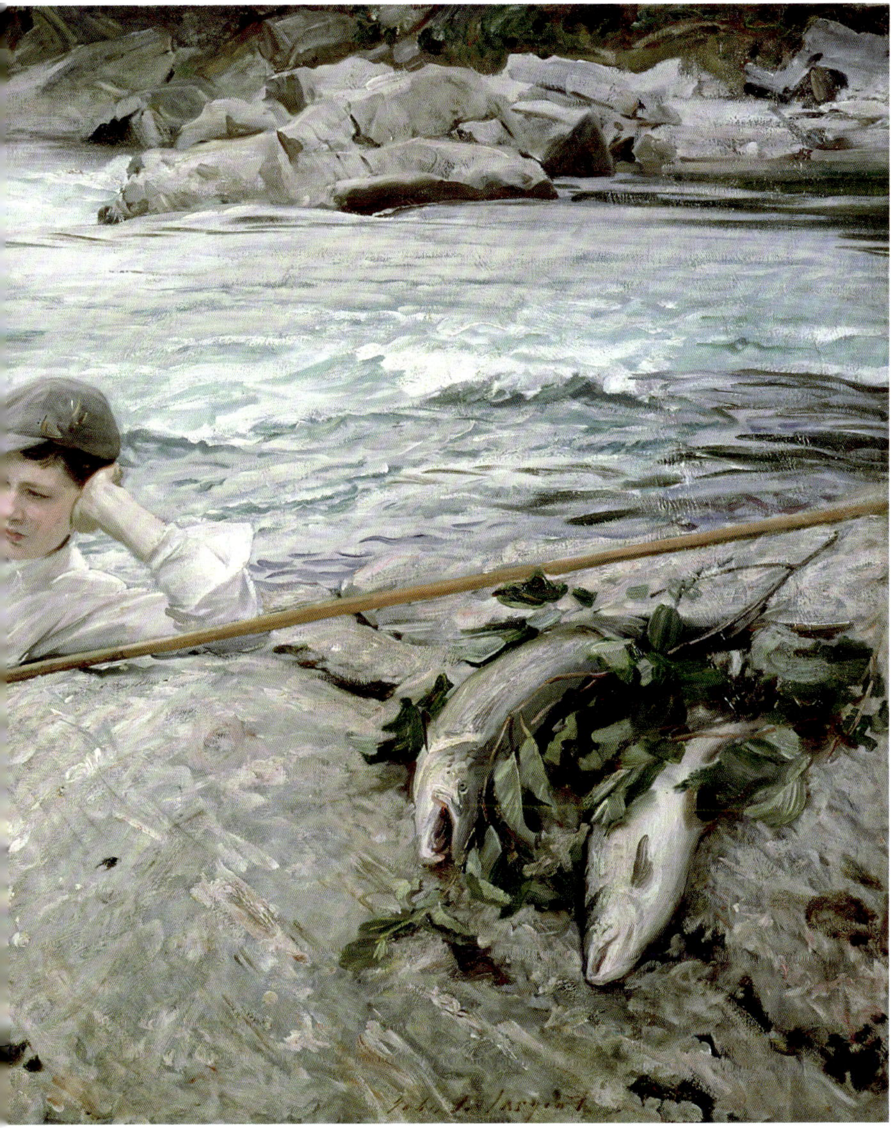

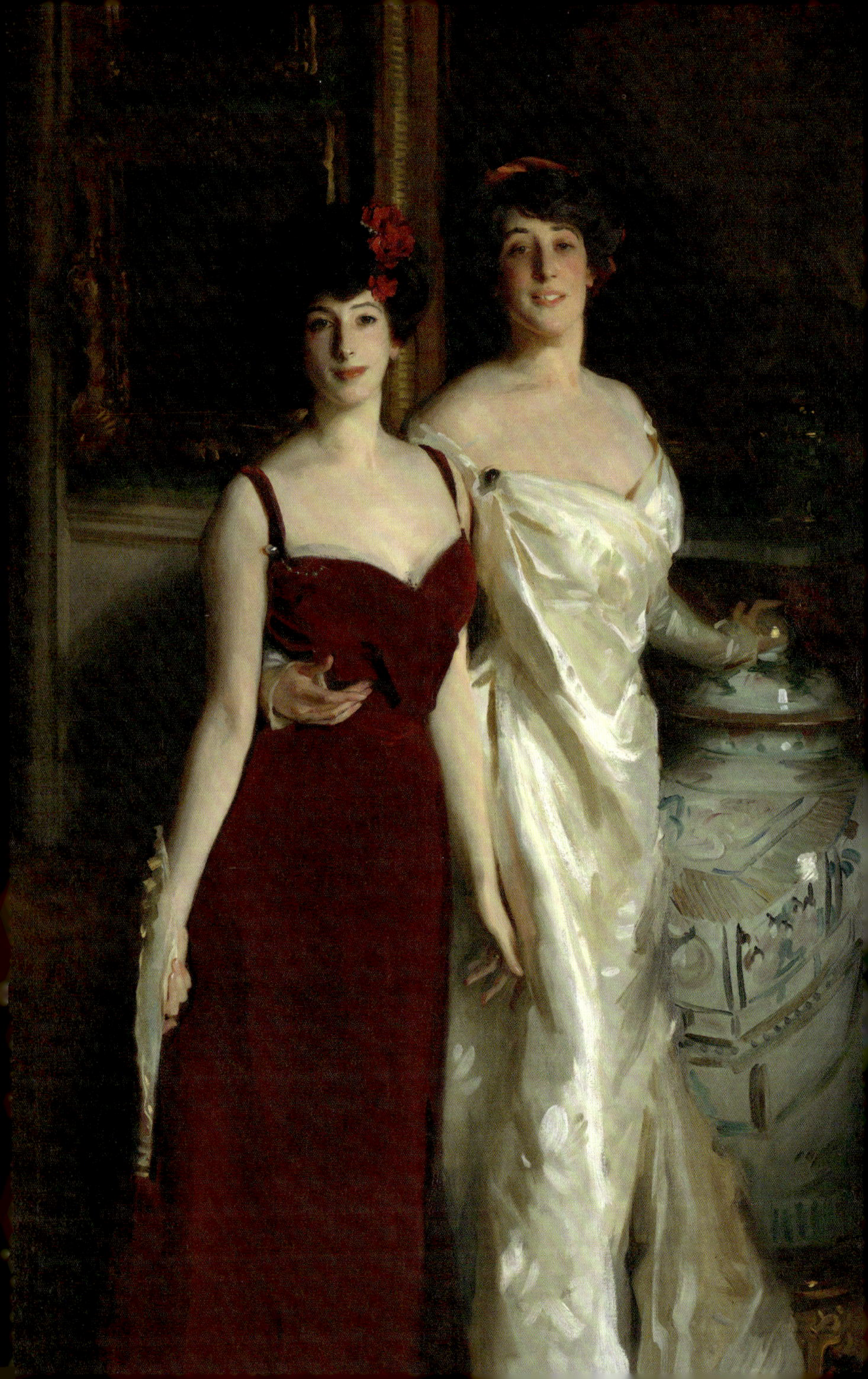

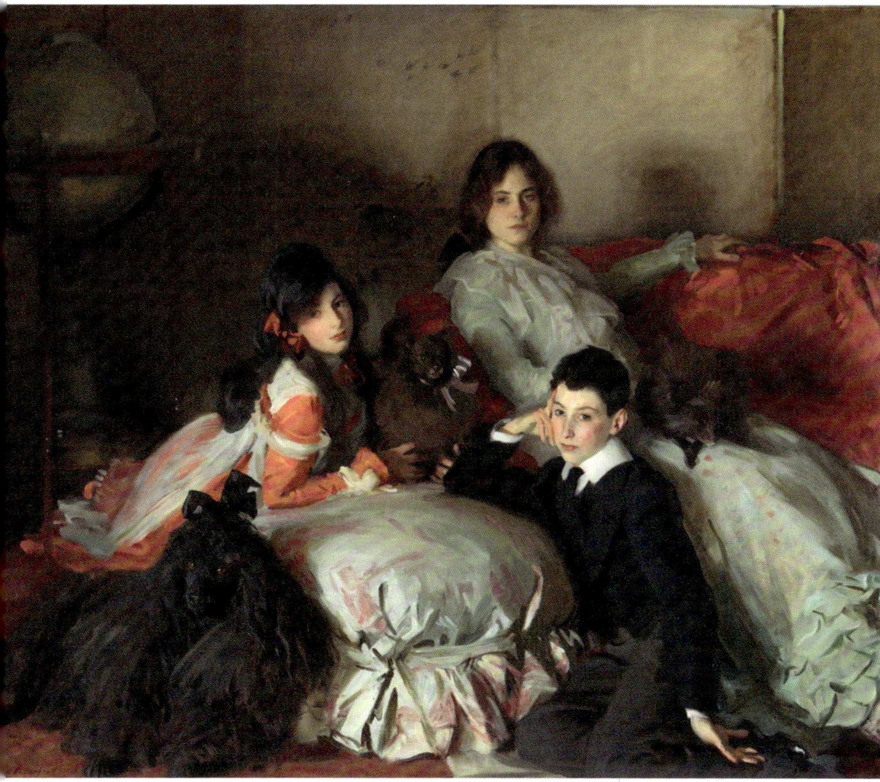

ıa and Betty, Daughters
' Asher and Mrs Wertheimer
)01
il paint on canvas
5.4 × 130.8

ssie, Ruby and Ferdinand,
ıildren of Asher Wertheimer
02
il paint on canvas
1.5 × 193.5

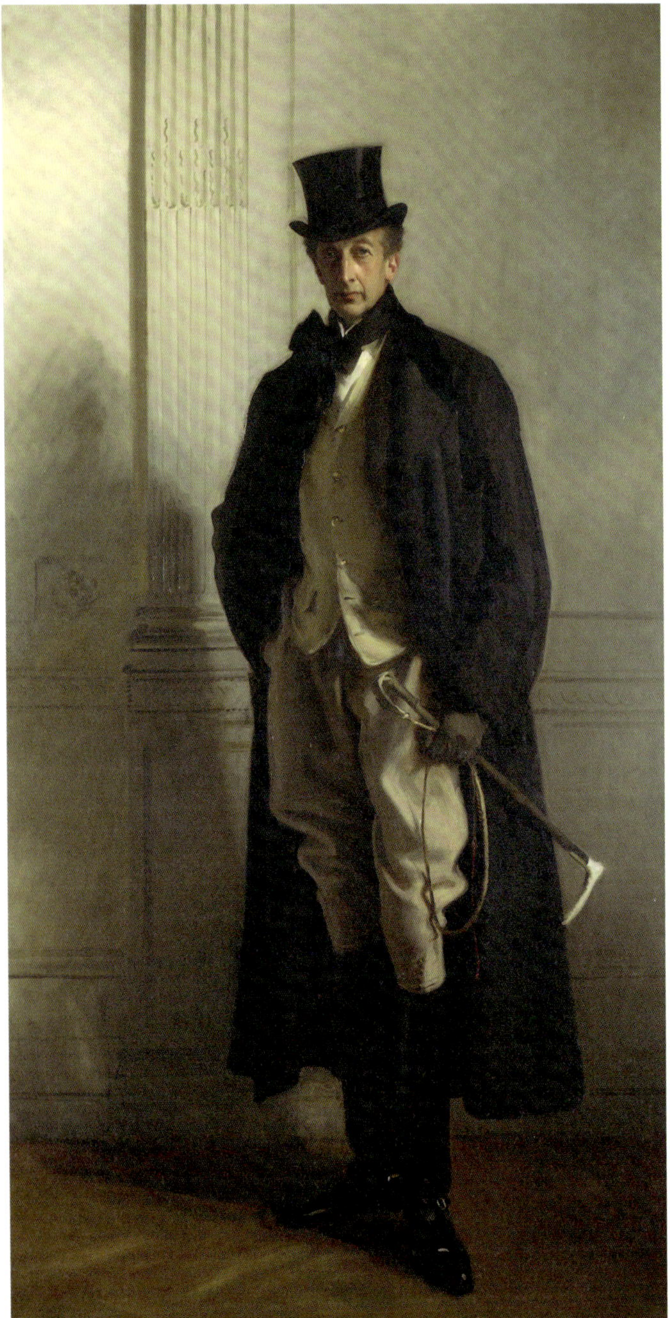

Lord Ribblesdale 1902
Oil paint on canvas
258.4 × 143.5

Sketch of Cellini's 'Perseus'
c.1902–6
Watercolour over graphite
on paper
36.5 × 22.9

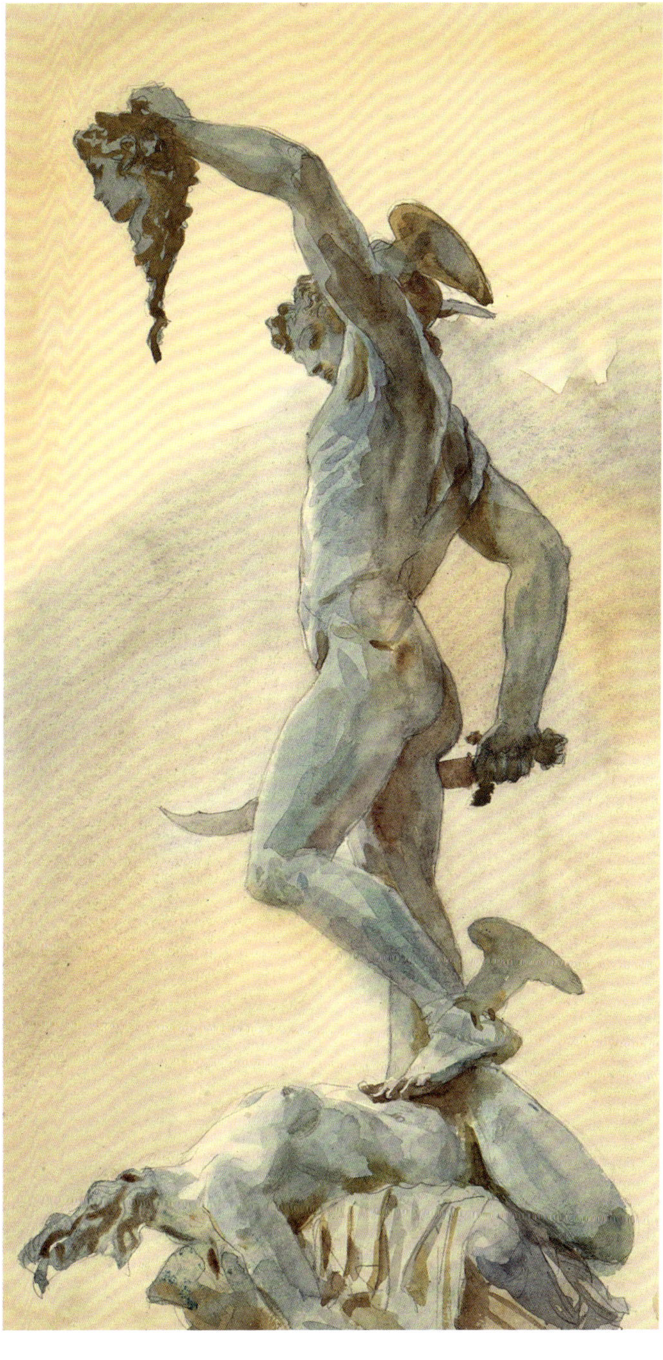

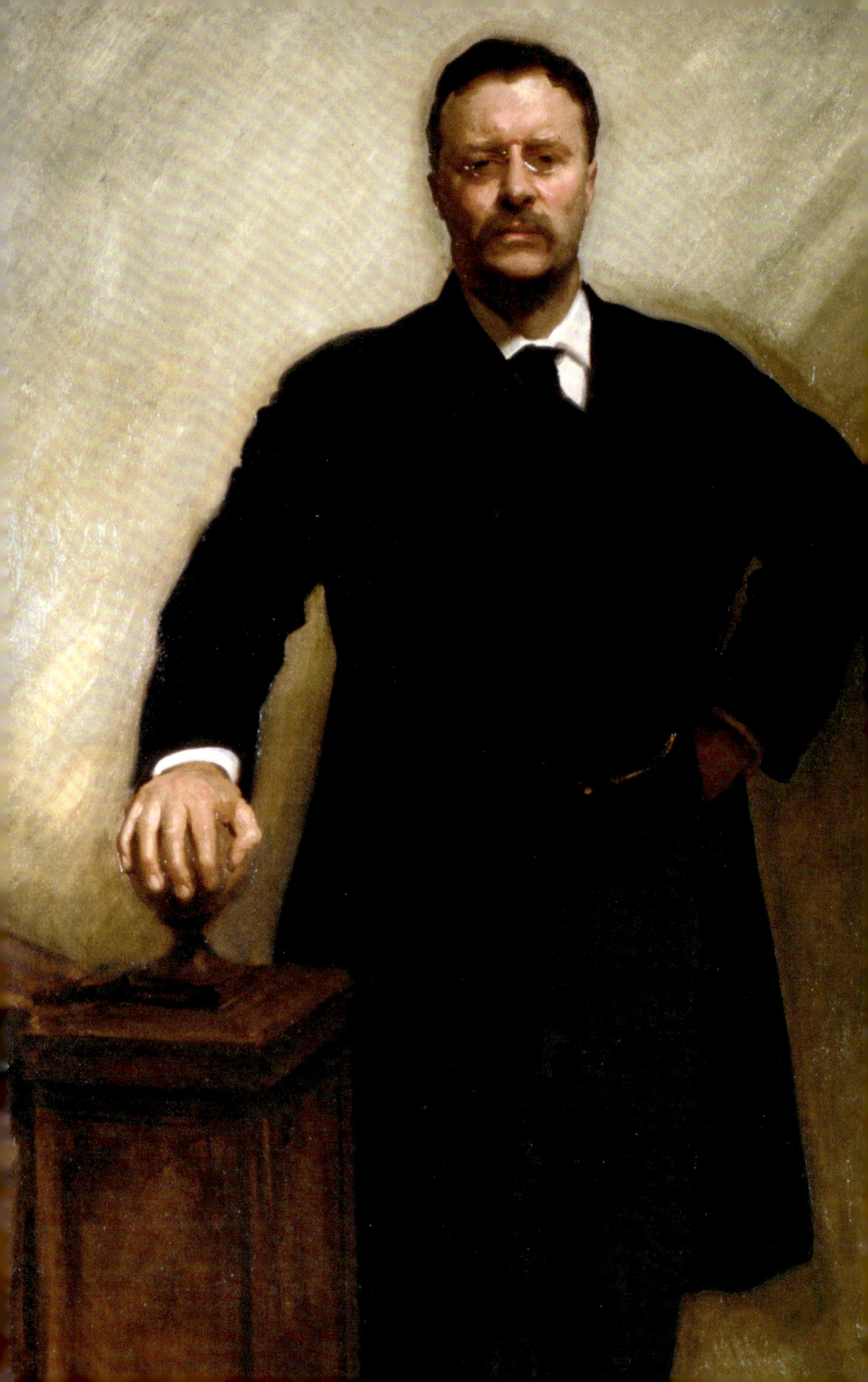

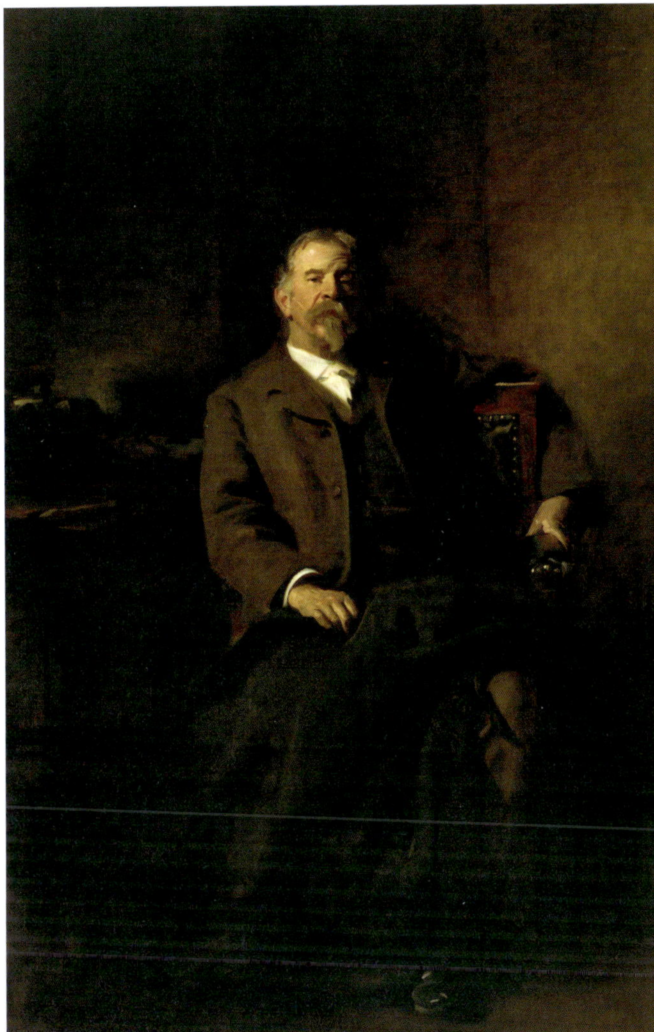

President Theodore Roosevelt
1903
Oil paint on canvas
147.3 × 101.6

Henry Lee Higginson 1903
Oil paint on canvas
245 × 153

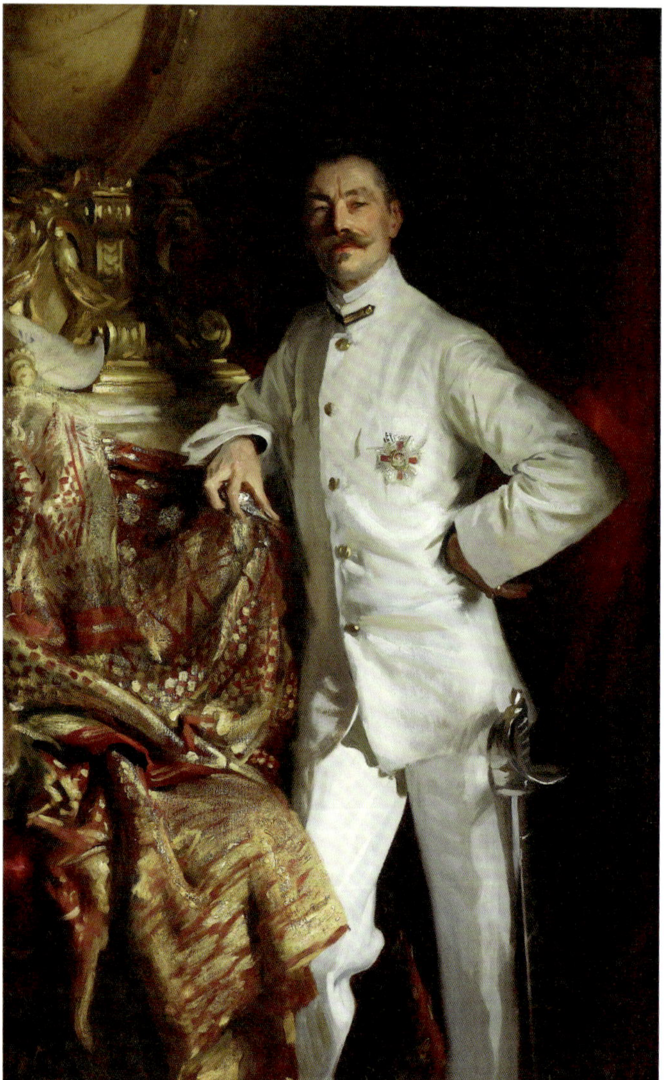

Sir Frank Swettenham 1904
Oil paint on canvas
170.8 × 110.5

The Marlborough Family
1904–5
Oil paint on canvas
287 × 238.7

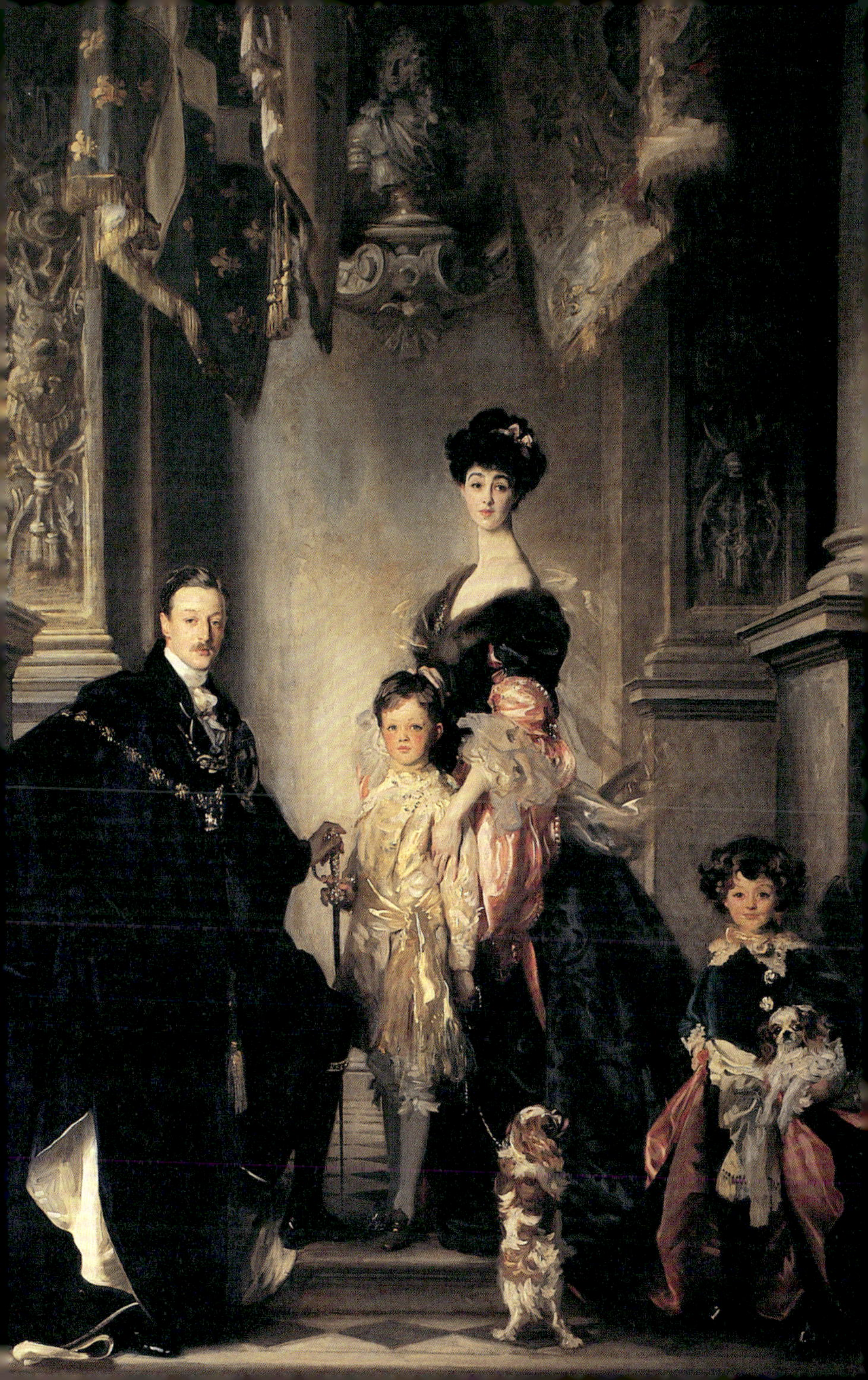

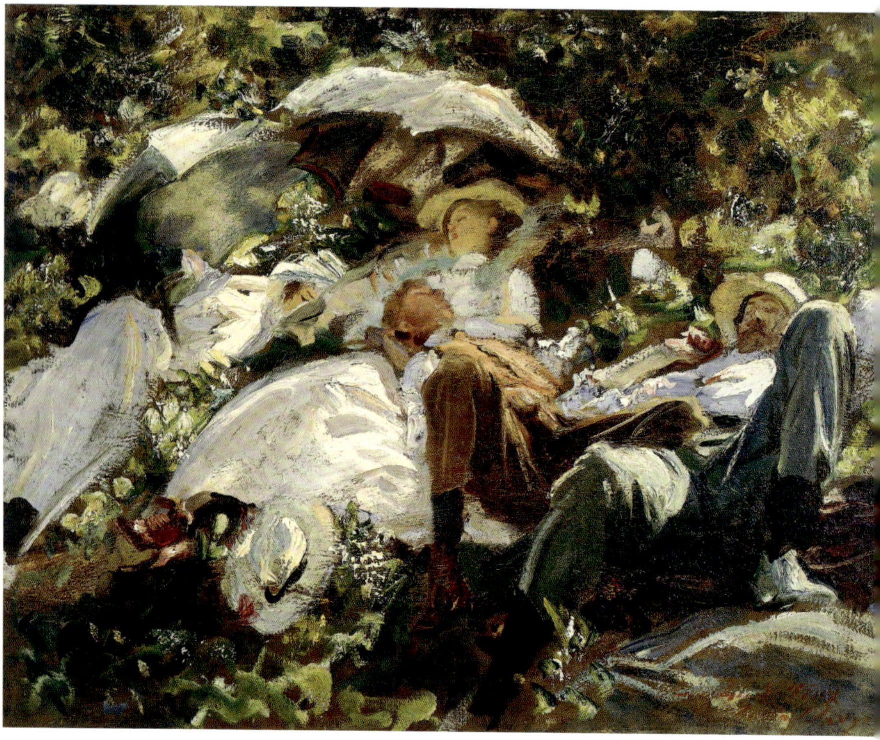

Group with Parasols
c.1904–5
Oil paint on canvas
55.3 × 70.8

Mrs Louis Raphael ?c.1906
Oil paint on canvas
149.8 × 99

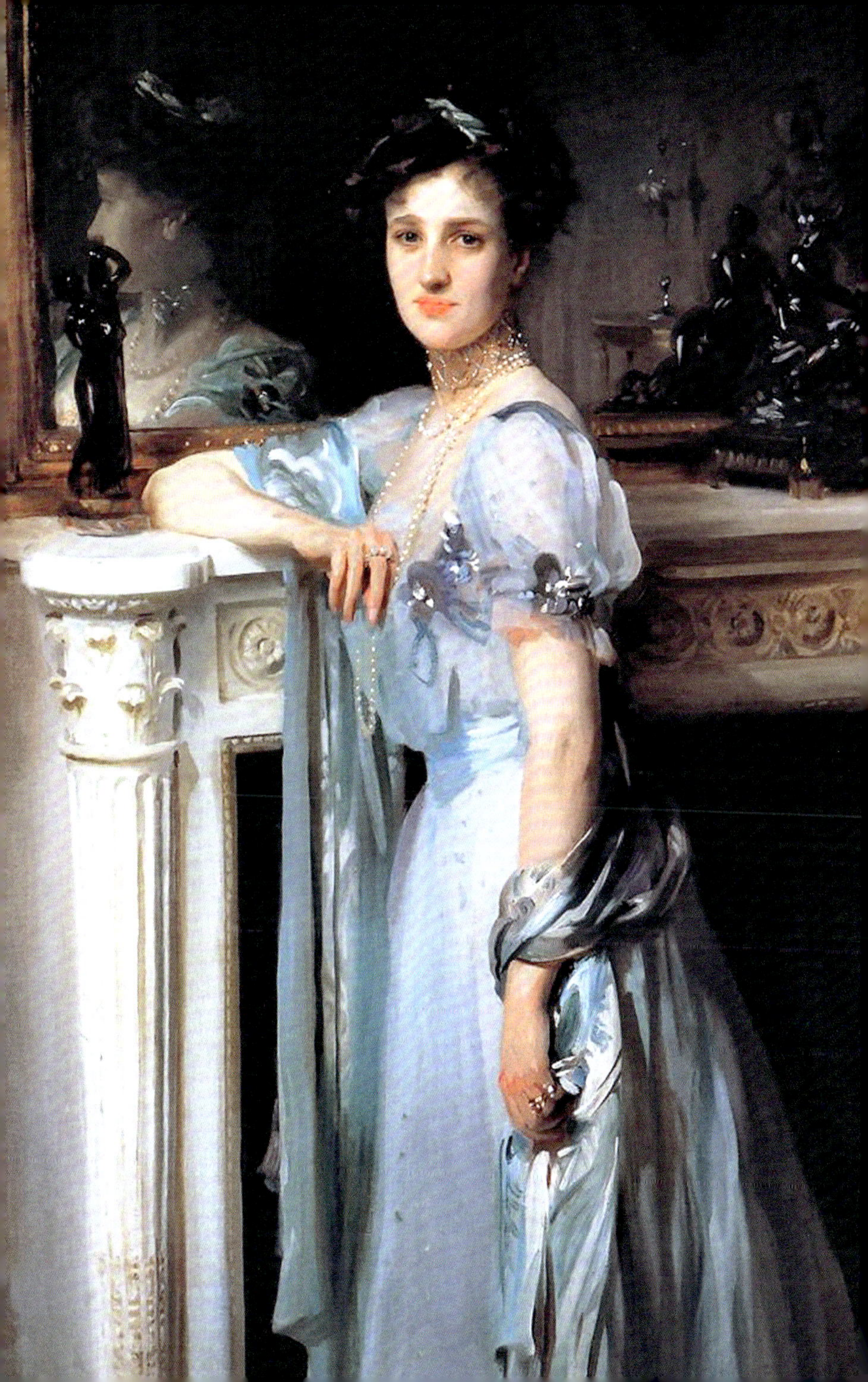

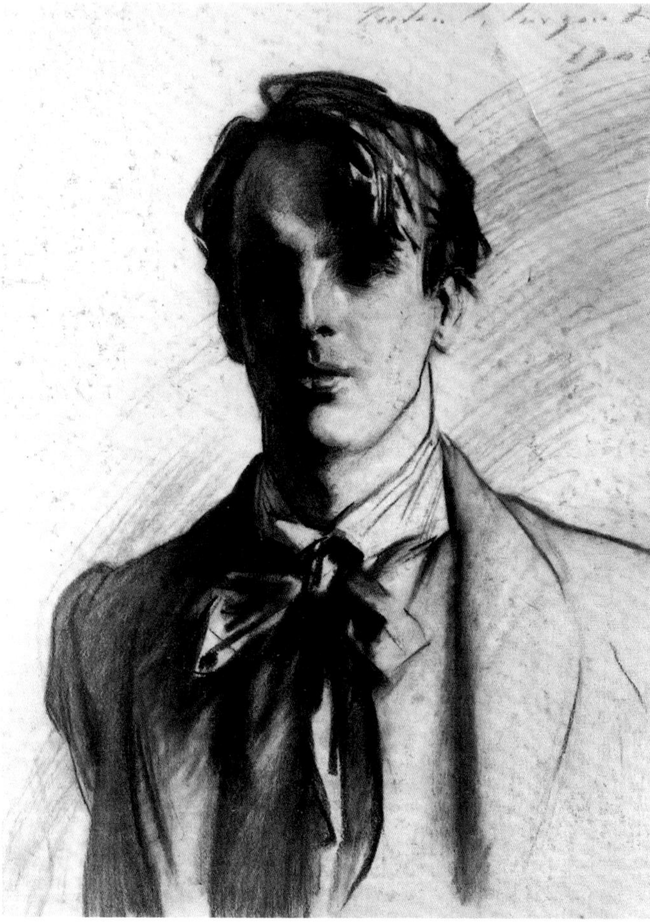

William Butler Yeats 1908
Charcoal on paper
62.2 × 47

Almina, Daughter of Asher Wertheimer 1908
Oil paint on canvas
134 × 98.5

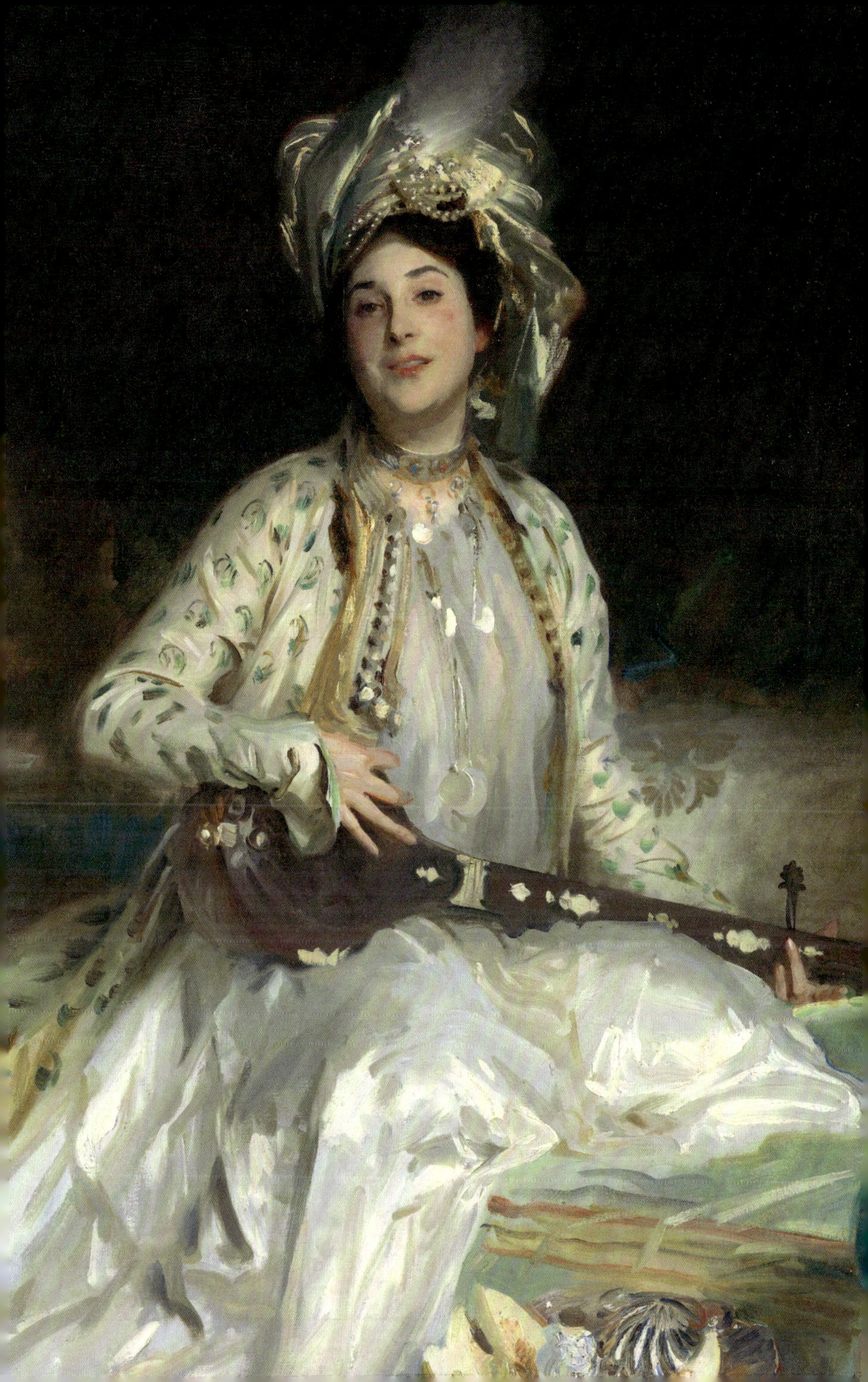

Cashmere c.1908
Oil paint on canvas
71.1 × 109.2

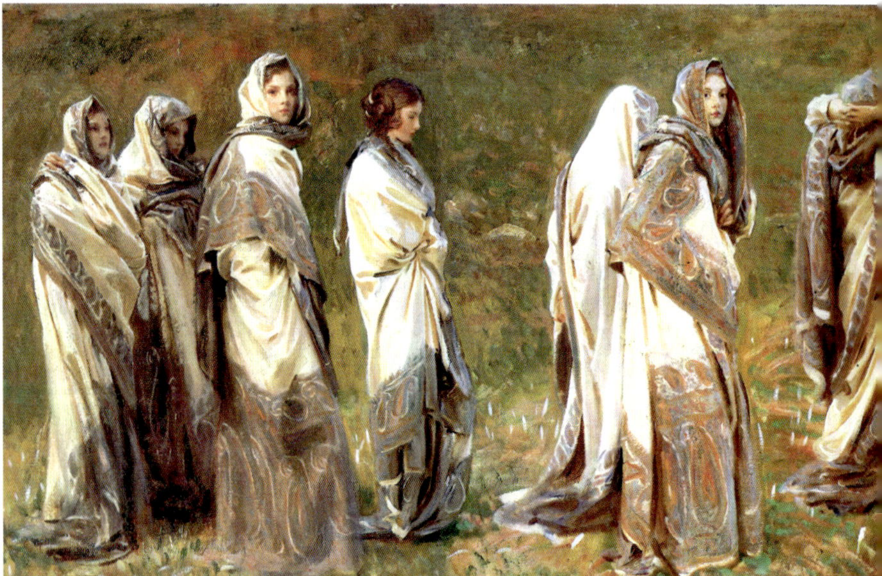

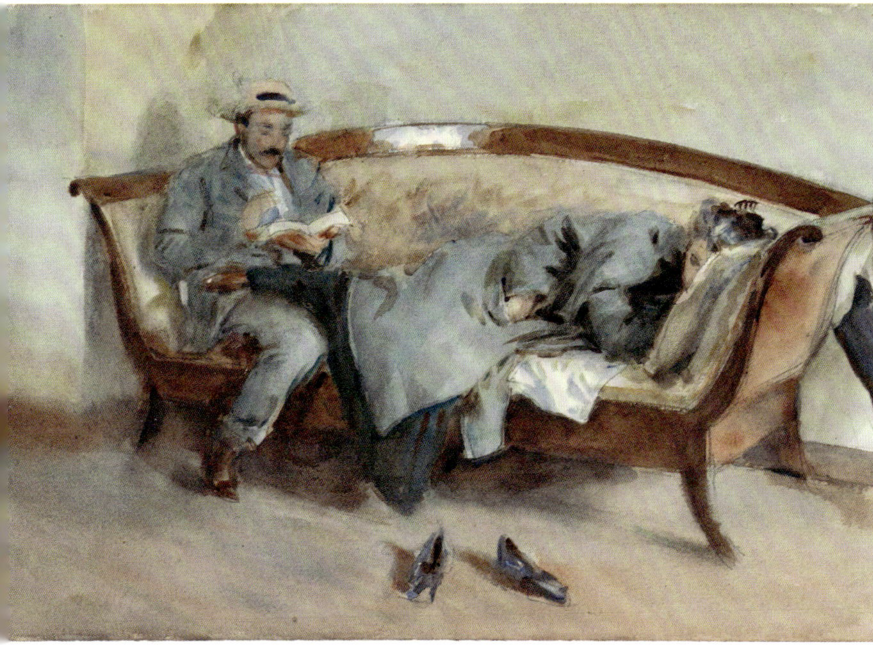

rfu: *A Rainy Day* 1909
atercolour over graphite
paper
.8 × 54

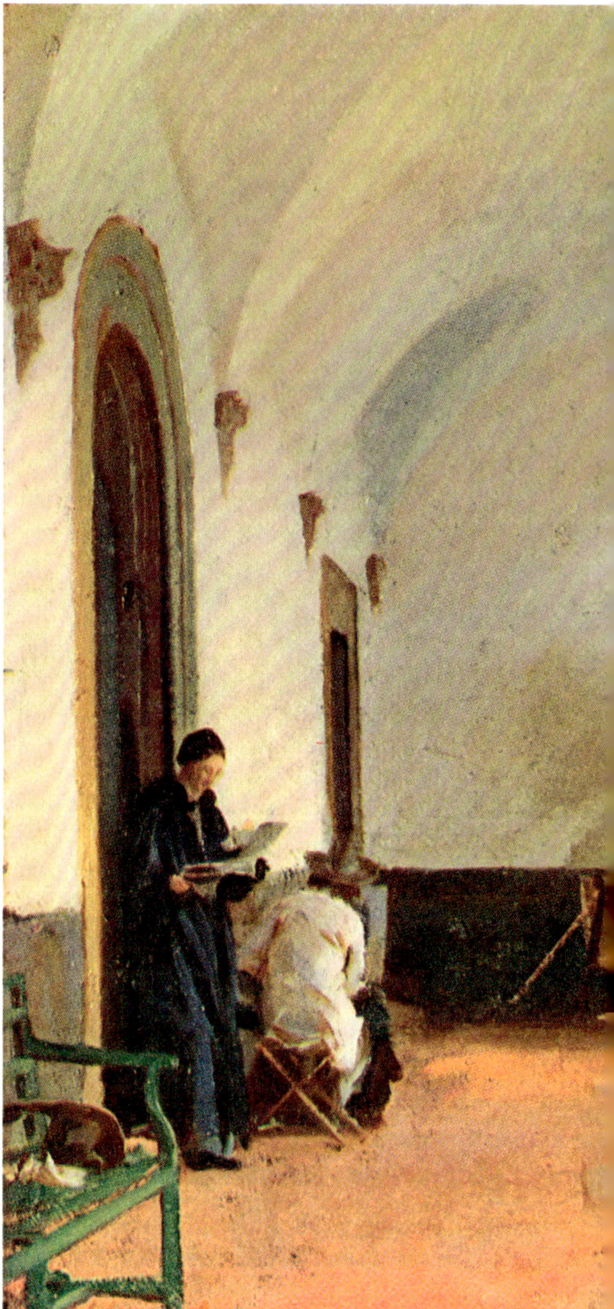

Villa Torre Galli: The Loggia
1910
Oil paint on canvas
55.9 × 71.1

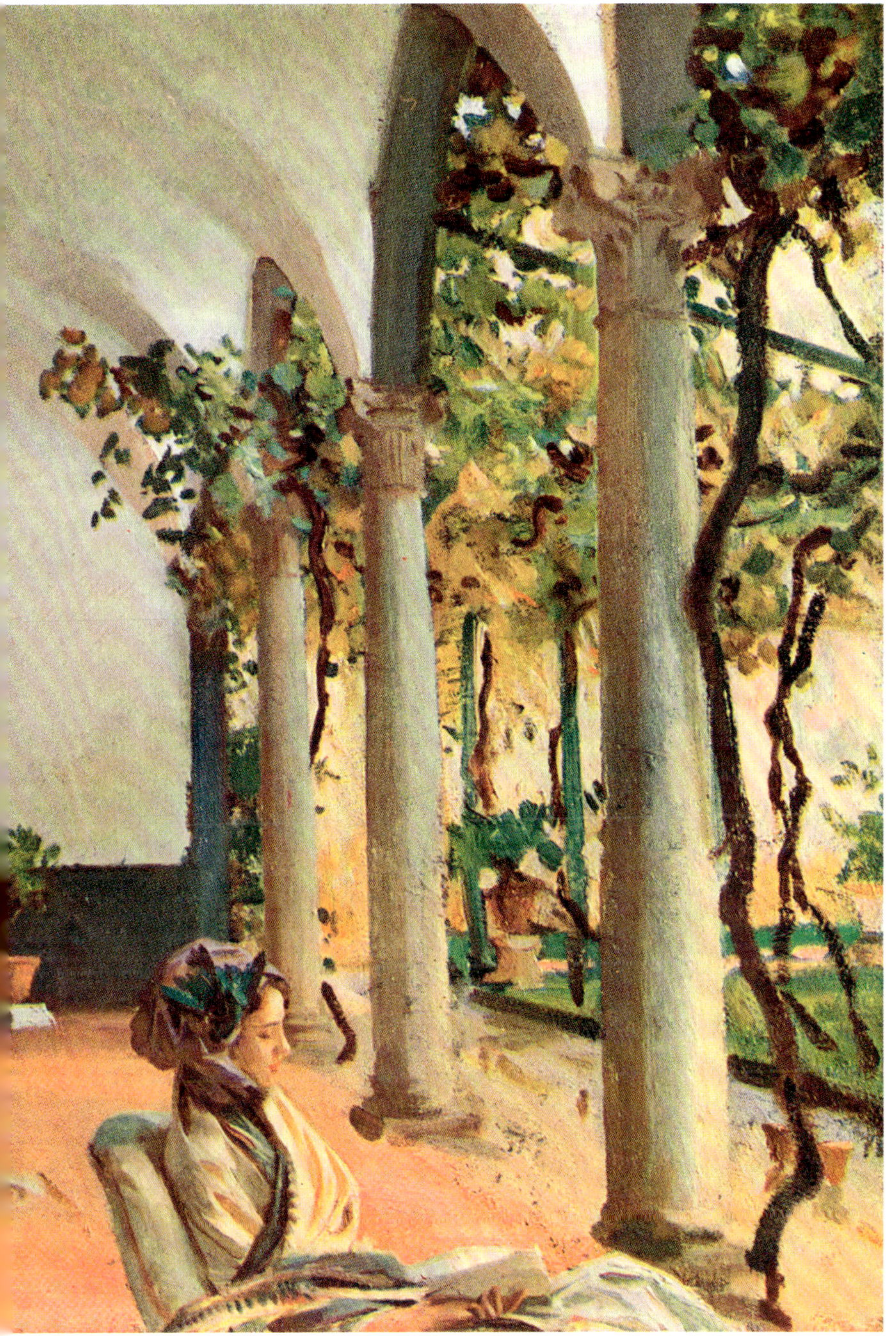

Nonchaloir 1911
Oil paint on canvas
63.8 × 76.2

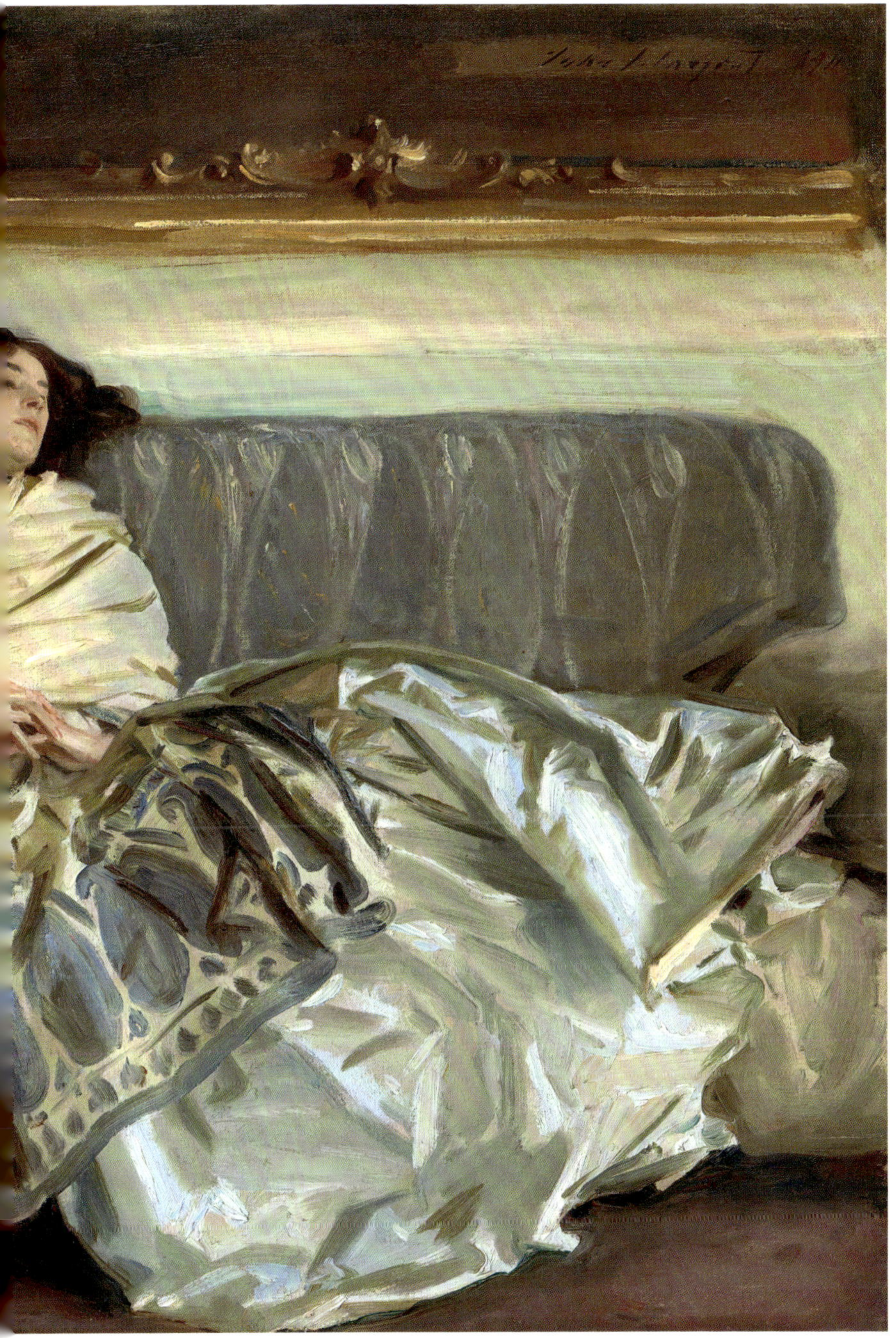

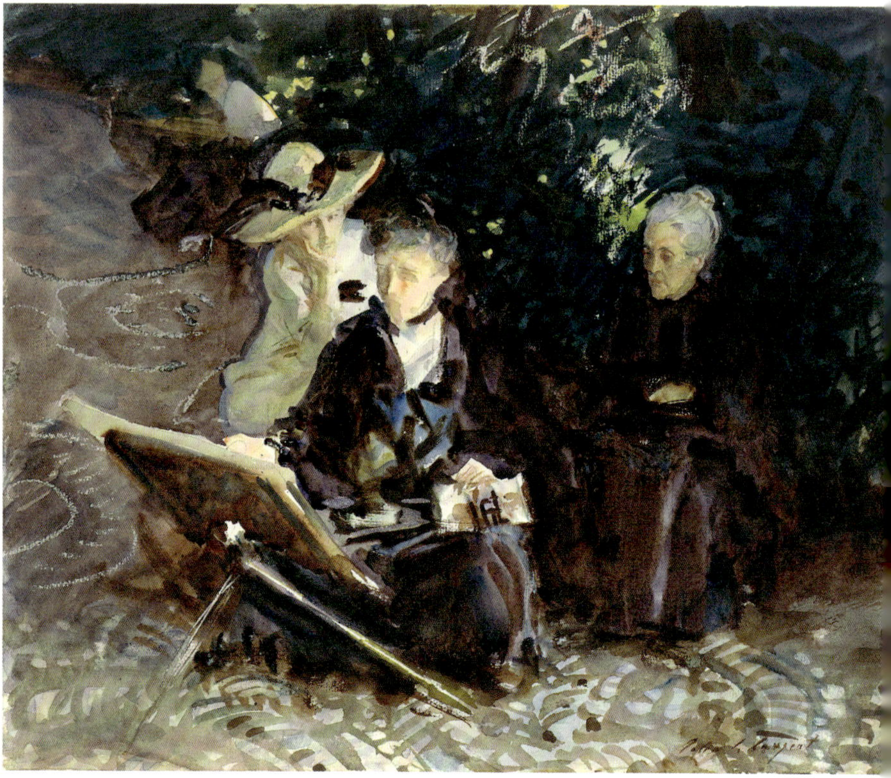

In the Generalife 1912
Watercolour over graphite
on paper
37.5 × 45.4

Spanish Fountain 1912
Watercolour over graphite,
with touches of body
colour, on paper
53.3 × 34.6

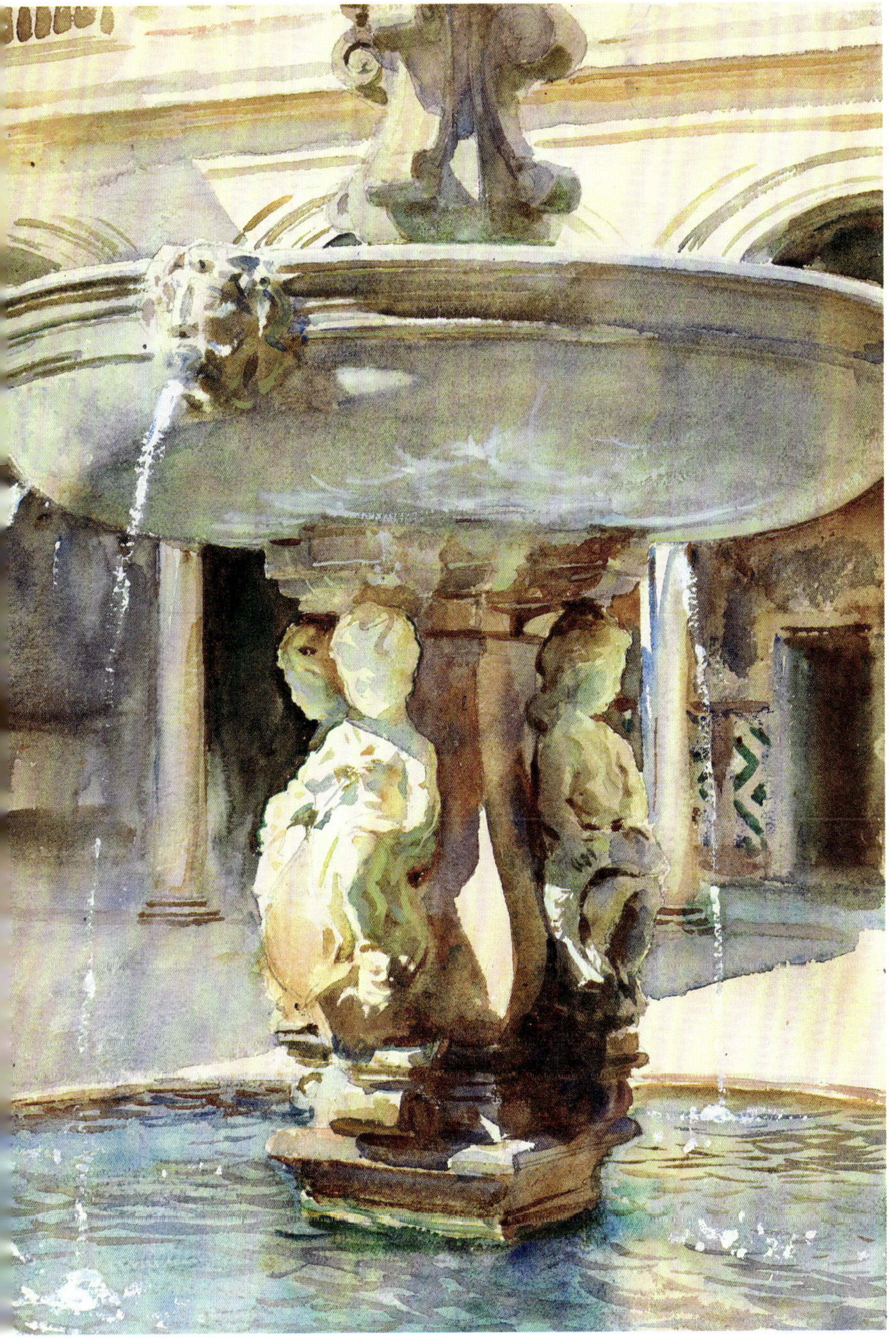

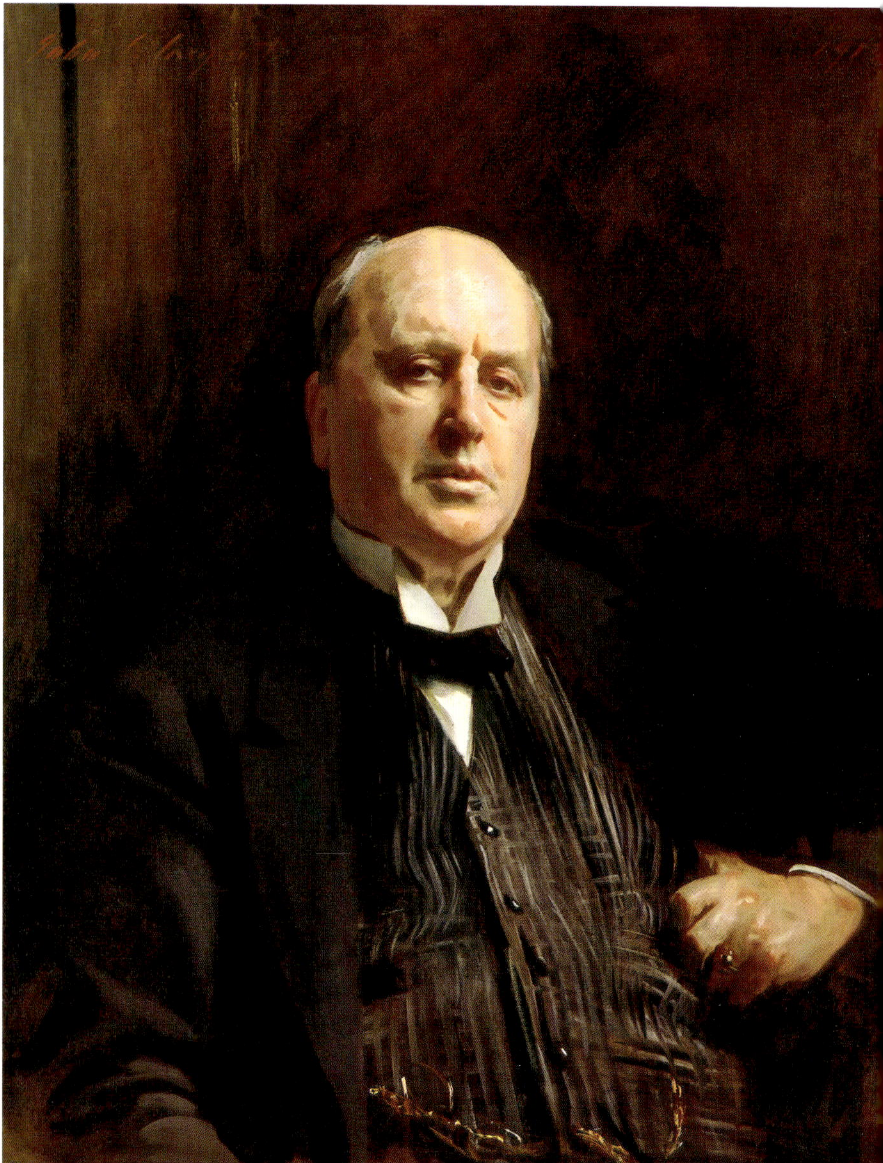

Henry James 1913
Oil paint on canvas
85.1 × 67.3

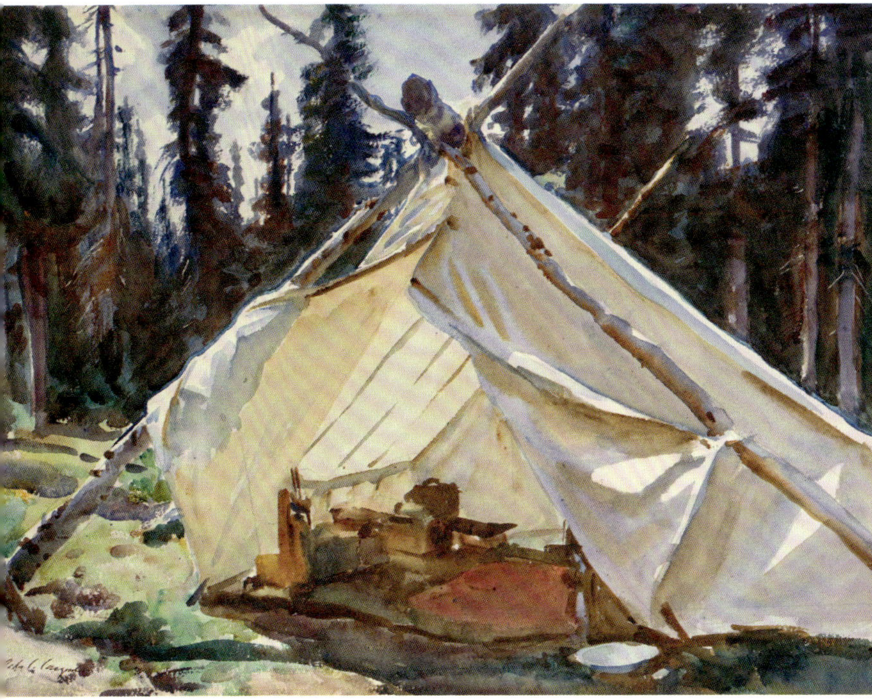

Tent in the Rockies c.1916
atercolour on paper
× 52

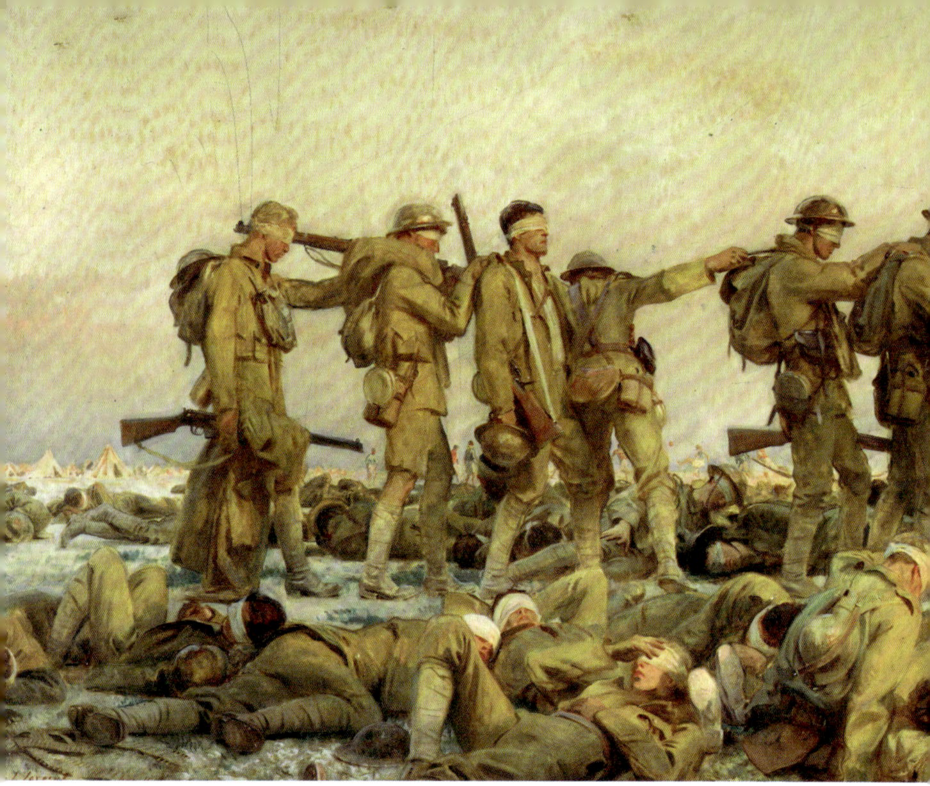

Gassed 1919
Oil paint on canvas
231 × 611.1

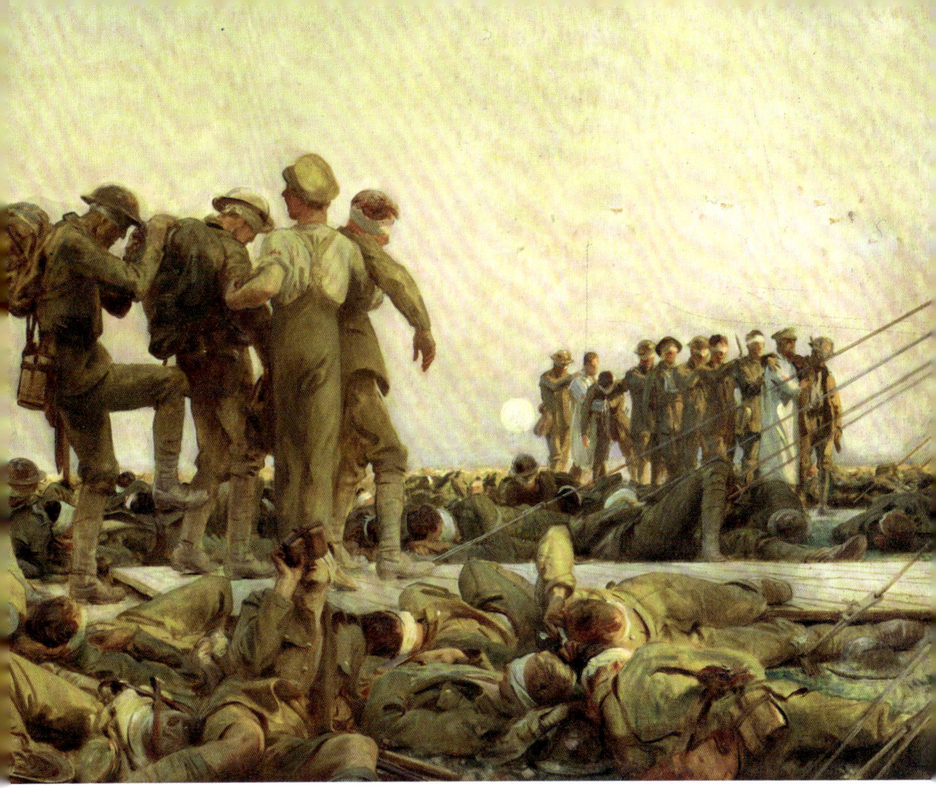

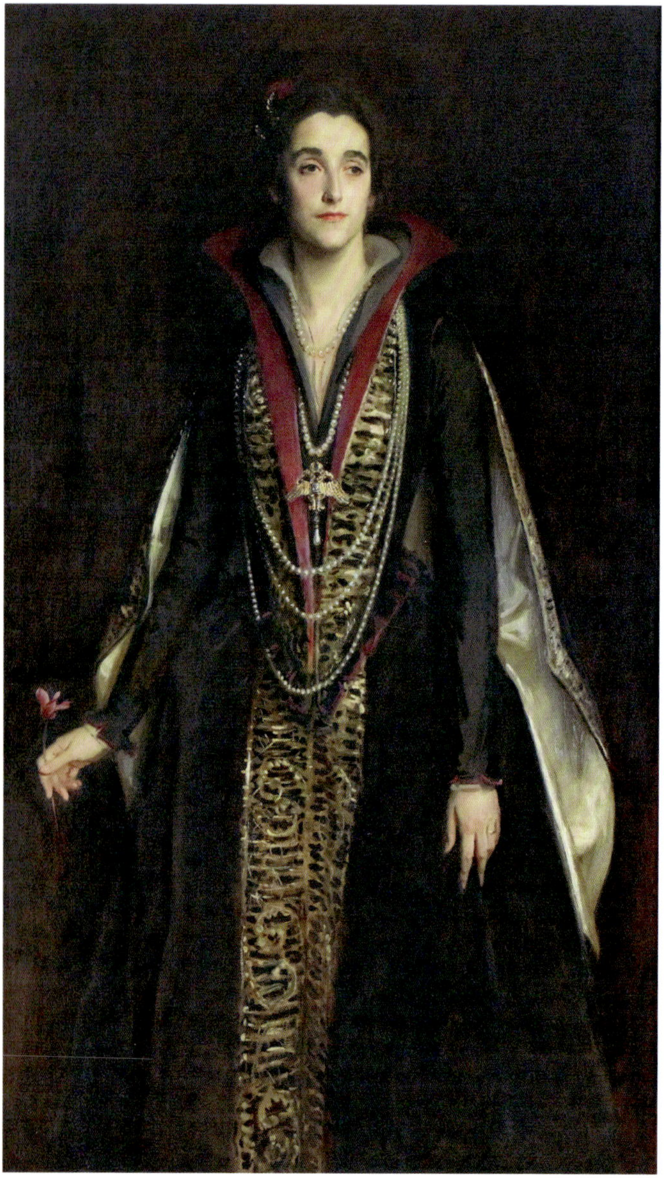

The Countess of Rocksavage
1922
Oil paint on canvas
161.3 × 89.8

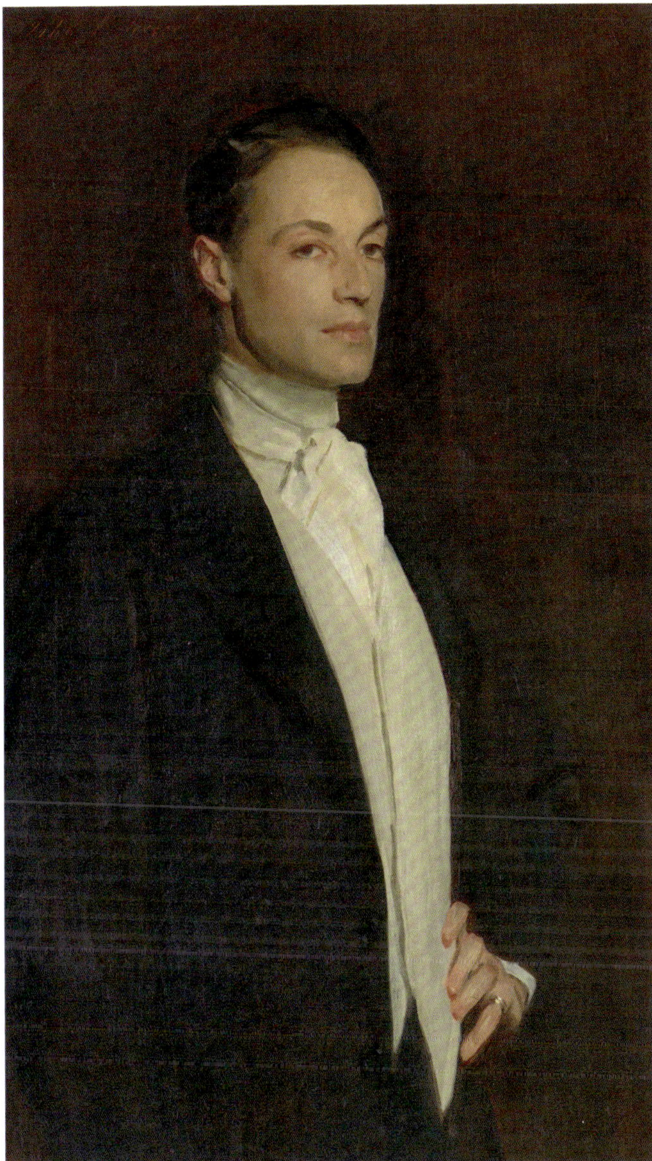

Sir Philip Sassoon 1923
Oil paint on canvas
95.2 × 57.8

NOTES

1. Vernon *Lee's Letters*, London 1937, p.765. Quoted in Richard Ormond and Elaine Kilmurray, *John Singer Sargent: Complete Paintings*, vol.1, New Haven and London 1998, p.76.

2. He also painted portraits of women she loved: A. Mary F. Robinson in 1881 and Clementina Anstruther-Thomson in 1889. See Ormond and Kilmurray 1998, pp.76–7, 220–2.

3. Vernon Lee, 'J.S.S.: In Memoriam', in Evan Charteris, *John Sargent*, London 1927, p.243.

4. See Sargent's letters to his friend Ben del Castillo, 23 May 1869, and his cousin Mrs Austin, 22 March 1874, reprinted in Charteris 1927, pp.12, 18.

5. The debut picture was a portrait of a family friend, *Frances Sherborne Ridley Watts* 1877 (Philadelphia Museum of Art).

6. John Singer Sargent, letter to Vernon Lee, 10 Feb. 1883, quoted in Ormond and Kilmurray 1998, p.113.

7. Dorothy Mahon and Silvia Centeno, 'A Technical Study of John Singer Sargent's Portrait of Madame Pierre Gautreau', *Metropolitan Museum Journal*, vol.40, 2005, pp.121–9.

8. On the dress, see Stephanie L. Herdrich, 'Madame X', in *Fashioned by Sargent*, exh. cat., Museum of Fine Arts Boston 2023, pp.35–9.

9. Charteris 1927, p.63.

10. Ibid., pp.61–2.

11. Ibid., p.65.

12. Ibid., p.173.

13. See Sally M. Promey, *Painting Religion in Public: John Singer Sargent's Triumph of Religion at the Boston Public Library*, Princeton, NJ 1999.

14. Charteris 1927, p.155.

15. On the social status of Sargent's sitters, see Elizabeth Prettejohn, *Interpreting Sargent*, London and New York 1998, pp.31–47, 55–8.

16. Charteris 1927, p.164. Sir George (a prominent lawyer) and Lady Lewis (born Elizabeth Eberstadt) had been friends of Sargent's since his earliest days in London.

17. See Kathleen Adler, 'Sargent's Portraits of the Wertheimer Family', in Linda Nochlin and Tamar Garb (eds.), *The Jew in the Text: Modernity and the Construction of Identity*, London 1995, pp.83–96; *John Singer Sargent: Portraits of the Wertheimer Family*, exh. cat., The Jewish Museum, New York 1999.

18. Henry James, 'Guildhall and Royal Academy' (1897), reprinted in *The Painter's Eye: Notes and Essays on the Pictorial Arts*, Madison, WI 1989, p.257.

19. See *Sargent: Portraits of Artists and Friends*, exh. cat., National Portrait Gallery, London 2015.

20. Letters quoted in Ormond and Kilmurray 1998, pp.167–8.

21. Charteris 1927, p.151.

22. *John Singer Sargent: The Sensualist*, exh. cat., Seattle Art Museum 2000.

23. Caroline Corbeau-Parsons and Rebecca Hellen, 'Ellen Terry as Lady Macbeth', in *Fashioned by Sargent*, exh. cat, Museum of Fine Arts Boston 2023, pp.105–11.

24. Ibid.

25. Henry James, 'John S. Sargent' (1887), reprinted in James 1989, pp.219, 217.

26. See Bruce Redford, *John Singer Sargent and the Art of Allusion*, New Haven and London 2016.

27. See John Collier, *The Art of Portrait Painting*, London 1910, pp.50–2.

28. Charteris 1927, p.158.

29. Collier 1910, pp.31, 75.

30. Charteris 1927, pp.181–2.

31. Reported by Mr Haley, a student at the RA Schools, in Charteris 1927, p.187.

32. W. Graham Robertson, *Time Was: The Reminiscences of W. Graham Robertson*, London 1931, pp.233, 238.

33. Vernon Lee in Charteris 1927, p.254 (punctuation amended for clarity).

INDEX

Page references in *italics* indicate images.

Agnew of Lochnaw, Lady 15, 56
Almina, Daughter of Asher Wertheimer 16, 79
Anderson, Elizabeth Garr[...] 15, 64
Asher Wertheimer 16, 57

Boston Public Library murals 14, 14–15, 24, 2[...]

Capri Girl on a Rooftop 10, 30[...]
Carnation, Lily, Lily, Rose 13, 46
Carolus-Duran 8, 9–10
Cashmere 22, 80
Cellini's 'Perseus', Sketch of 15, 71
The Children of Israel Beneath the Yoke of their Oppressors 14 15
Claude Monet Painting by the Edge of a Wood 9, 13, 44
Corfu: A Rainy Day 15, 81
The Countess of Rocksavage 15, 92

The Daughters of Edward D. Boit 10, 41
Dorothy Barnard 50
Dr Pozzi or Dr Pozzi at Home 13, 15, 40
Durand, Charles-Émile-Auguste 8, 9–10

El Jaleo 10, 36–7
Elizabeth Garrett Anderson 15, 64
Ellen Terry as Lady Macbeth 15, 22, 49
Elsie Palmer 15, 53
Ena and Betty, Daughters of Asher and Mrs Wertheime[...] 16, 68
Essie, Ruby and Ferdinand, Children of AsherWerthei[...] 16, 69

Fauré, Gabriel 15, 20, 52
Fête Familiale or The Birthday Party 13, 45
Fumée d'ambre gris 10, 35
Gabriel Fauré 15, 20, 52

Gassed 24–5, 90–1
Gautreau, Madame 10–13,
Group with Parasols 76

elleu, Paul 13, 51
enry James 14, 88
enry Lee Higginson 15, 73
omer Saint-Gaudens and his Mother 15, 54
e Honourable Mrs Charles Russell 63
e Honourable Victoria Stanley 15, 61

the Generalife 15, 86
e Interior of a Hospital Tent 25, 25
Interior in Venice 58–9
elin, Mrs Adrian 15, 48

mes, Henry 14, 18, 22, 88

dy Agnew of Lochnaw 15, 56
dy Elcho, Mrs Adeane and Mrs Tennant or The Wyndham Sisters 15, 62
s Hilanderas, after Velázquez 22, 34
e, Vernon 4, 5–6, 25
rd Ribblesdale 16, 70

adame Édouard Pailleron 10, 32
adame X or Madame Gautreau 10–13, 11
e Marlborough Family 15–16, 75
cKeller, Thomas E. 21, 21
eyer family 17, 18
e Misses Vickers 42–3
onet, Claude 9, 13, 44
rs Adrian Iselin 15, 48
rs Carl Meyer and her Children 17, 18
s Charles Thursby 60
rs Edward Davis and her Son, Livingston 55
s Louis Raphael 77
ural painting 14, 14 15, 24, 25

apolitan Children Bathing 10, 31
nchaloir 84–5
ude Study of Thomas E. McKeller 21, 21

n his Holidays, Norway 66–7
yster Gatherers of Cancale 10, 28–9

ailleron, Mme Édouard 10, 32
e Pailleron Children 10, 39
ul Helleu Sketching with his Wife or An Out-of-Doors Study 13, 51

portraiture 9–10, 14, 15–16
and friendship 18–22
Jewish sitters 16–18
Pozzi, Dr Samuel Jean 13, 15, 40
President Theodore Roosevelt 15, 72

Rehearsal of the Pasdeloup Orchestra at the Cirque d'Hiver 33
Ribblesdale, Lord 16, 70
Robert Louis Stevenson and his Wife 19–20, 20
Robertson, W. Graham 23
Roosevelt, Theodore 15, 72
Russell, Mrs Charles 63
Ruth Sears Bacon 47

Saint-Gaudens family 15, 54
Salon, Paris 9, 10, 12
Sargent, John Singer
training in Paris 9–10
childhood 6–9
in England and America 13–16
studio practice and technique 22–4
Self-Portrait 19, 19
Sir Frank Swettenham 15, 74
Sir George Sitwell, Lady Ida Sitwell and Family 15, 65
Sir Philip Sassoon 93
Sitwell family 15, 65
Spanish Fountain 87
Stanley, Victoria 15, 61
Stevenson, Robert Louis 19–20, 20
Swettenham, Sir Frank 15, 74

A Tent in the Rockies 15, 24, 89
Two Octopi 10, 26

Venetian Interior 38
Vernon Lee 4, 5–6
Villa Torre Galli: The Loggia 82–3
Violet Sargent or The Breakfast Table 6, 7

W. Graham Robertson 23
Wertheimer portraits 16, 57, 68, 69, 79
Whistler, James Abbott McNeill 13, 15
William Butler Yeats 15, 78
Wyndham sisters 15, 62

Yeats, W.B. 15, 78

CREDITS

The Alfred Beit Foundation, Russborough House 34

The Armand Hammer Collection. Gift of the Armand Hammer Foundation. Hammer Museum, Los Angeles 40

Blenheim Palace, Oxfordshire, UK / Bridgeman Images 75

Brooklyn Museum, Museum Collection Fund, 20.640 51

Carnegie Museum of Art, Pittsburgh, PA / Art Resource, NY 38, 54

Collection of the Colorado Springs Fine Arts Center at Colorado College. Museum purchase through Debutante Ball Purchase Fund. FA 1969.3.1.53

Crystal Bridges Museum of American Art, Bentonville, Arkansas 20, 30

Des Moines Art Center. Photo credit: Rich Sanders, Des Moines 39

© The Fitzwilliam Museum, University of Cambridge 50, 87

Fogg Art Museum, Cambridge, Massachusetts. Photo credit: © President and Fellows of Harvard College 7

Galleria degli Uffizi, Collezione degli Autoritratti, Florence. Photo Scala, Florence. Courtesy of the Ministero Beni e Att. Culturali e del Turismo 19

Harvard University Portrait Collection. Gift by student subscription to the Harvard Union, 1903. Photo © President and Fellows of Harvard College, H189 73

Isabella Stewart Gardner Museum, Boston 89

Photo © Isabella Stewart Gardner Museum / Bridgeman Images front cover 36-7

Imperial War Museum, London © IWM 25,90-1

Boston Public Library © Photography Sheryl Lanzel 14

Los Angeles County Museum of Art, CA, USA / Bridgeman Images 55

© The Metropolitan Museum of Art / Art Resource / Scala, Florence 11, 62, 86

Photo © Minneapolis Institute of Art / The Ethel Morrison Van Derlip Fund and the John R. Van Derlip Fund / Bridgeman Images 45

Montgomery Museum of Fine Arts, Alabama / Photo: Painters/ Alamy 77

Musée de la Musique, Paris / Photo: Heritage Image Partnership / Alamy 52

Museum of Fine Arts, Boston. All rights reserved / Scala, Florence 21, 33, 41, 81

© The National Gallery, London 70

National Gallery of Art, Washington 28-9, 32, 48, 71, 84-5

© National Galleries of Scotland 56

© National Museums Liverpool / Bridgeman Images 66-7

© National Portrait Gallery, London 74, 88 / Private collection 64

Newark Museum of Art. Purchase by exchange, 1985. Gift of Mr. and Mrs. Duncan Pitney, Emilie Coles from the J. Ackerman Coles Collection, Mrs. Lewis B. Ballantine, Mrs. Owen Winston, and the Bequest of Louis Bamberger 60

Private collection 61, 63, 78, 80 / Alamy / Painters 26

Private collection / Photo © Houghton Hall 92

Private collection / Photo Fine Art Images / Heritage Images / Scala, Florence 76, 82-3

© Royal Academy of Arts, London 58-9

Sheffield City Art Galleries. Bequest of Douglas Vickers 1938 © Sheffield Museums Trust 42-3

Sterling and Francine Clark Art Institute, Williamstown, Massachusetts 2, 8, 31, 35

© Tate, 2024 4, 17, 23, 44, 46, 49, 57, 68-9, 79, 93

Wadsworth Atheneum, Hartford, Connecticut (1975.92) / Photo Allen Phillips / Wadsworth Atheneum 47

The White House, Washington, D.C © 2024 White House Historical Association 72

The publishers have made every effort to trace the copyright holders of the works illustrated and apologise for any omissions or errors that may have been made.

First published 2024 by order of the Tate Trustees by Tate Publishing, a division of Tate Enterprises Ltd, Millbank, London SW1P 4RG
www.tate.org.uk/publishing

Reprinted 2024, 2025

A catalogue record for this book is available from the British Library

ISBN 978 1 84976 902 0

Distributed in the United States and Canada by ABRAMS, New York

Library of Congress Control Number applied for

Senior Editor: Emma Poulter
Production: Bill Jones
Picture Researcher: Emma O'Neill
Designed by Astrid Stavro
Colour reproduction by DL Imaging, London
Printed and bound in Italy by Printer Trento S.r.l

Cover: *El Jaleo* c.1880–2 (detail, see pp.36–7)
Frontispiece: *Fumée d'ambre gris* 1880 (detail, see p.35)

Measurements of artworks are given in centimetres, height before width and depth

FSC www.fsc.org MIX Paper | Supporting responsible forestry FSC® C015829

ABOUT THE AUTHOR
Elizabeth Prettejohn is a writer, independent curator and Professor of History of Art at the University of York.